RAMEN

FUSION

COOKBOOK

RAMEN FUSION COOKBOOK

Nell Benton

Publisher: Mike Sanders
Associate Publisher: Billy Fields
Executive Acquisitions Editor: Nathalie Mornu
Cover and Book Designer: XAB Design
Photographer: Michael Berman
Food Stylist: Laura Kinsey-Dolph
Development Editor: Kayla Dugger
Compositor: Ayanna Lacey
Proofreader: Monica Stone
Indexer: Heather McNeill

First American Edition, 2015
Published in the United States by DK Publishing
6081 E. 82nd Street, Indianapolis, Indiana, 46250

www.dk.com

A WORLD OF IDEAS
SEE ALL THERE IS TO KNOW

CONTENTS

¥300 あったか～い ¥300 あったか～い ¥300 あったか～い ¥3 あった

INTRODUCTION TO RAMEN

What is the ramen obsession all about? This Japanese soul-food dish has been popping up all over the world, as ramen enthusiasts re-create and build upon the traditional bowl of ramen. By knowing the history and techniques behind ramen, you can start to embrace this truly special dish.

A BACKGROUND ON RAMEN

Forget the high-sodium packet noodles you subsisted on in college. Strictly speaking, ramen is noodles, broth, and toppings. The finished result yields a simple, delicious, and beautiful bowl of ramen—and a labor of love, from start to finish.

1900
Ramen originally came from China, as a variation of a dish called *lamian.* The exact date is unknown, but there's a consensus that prior to World War II, ramen shops established by Chinese immigrants existed in Japan.

1958
In 1958, Momofuku Ando invented instant ramen, which was sold in **little bricks wrapped in colorful plastic packaging**. They were made by flash-frying cooked noodles, which were later rehydrated with hot water.

1985
The movie *Tampopo,* a Japanese comedy, tells the story of two truck drivers who teach a ramen shop owner how to improve her fare. It contains scenes on how to eat ramen properly, as well as the love that must go into making the broth.

1945
After the war, many Japanese soldiers returned home from China with an appreciation for lamian, and some quickly established **eateries with ramen on the menu**.

1971
Taking his creation one step further, in 1971, Momofuku Ando invented the **heat-resistant instant noodle cup** made of Styrofoam, which could be used to rehydrate the noodles without ever taking them out of the package.

1999
The Momofuku Ando Instant Ramen Museum opens in Osaka, Japan. It features a replica of the backyard shed in which Ando developed instant ramen and hands-on exhibits that allow visitors to make their own noodles.

2008
Ramen Girl, an American-made film, focuses on an American girl living in Japan who learns about the art of making ramen, as well as the power of redemption contained in a well-made bowl of noodles.

2015–
Ramen chefs in Japan continue to create new and exciting variations based on ingredients available to them in this global market (known as *fusion*).

1994
The **Shin-Yokohama Raumen Museum** opens in Yokohama, Japan. Devoted to ramen soup, this food amusement park included branches of famous ramen restaurants from across Japan.

2004
Chef David Chang opens his first noodle restaurant, **Momofuku Noodle Bar, in New York City**. Its inventiveness with ingredients is arguably what started the ramen craze outside of Japan.

2011
CupNoodles Museum opens in Yokohama, Japan. It includes a room with more than 3,000 ramen product packages and a "factory" where visitors can embellish a foam cup and fill it with their choice of ingredients and toppings.

RAMEN ACROSS JAPAN

Just like different parts of Italy are known for their distinct dishes, and different regions of France for their wines, the same holds true for ramen in Japan. Ramen varies greatly from region to region, depending on climate, tradition, outside influence, and the availability of ingredients. While there are too many regional varieties of ramen to list, here are five regions that should be added to any ramen pilgrimage!

KYOTO

Kyoto is known for its chicken-based broth. Highly *kotteri*, the ramen broth is generally even thicker than tonkotsu and is served with a thin, straight noodle, usually softer than the average ramen noodle. Toppings can include garlic, kujnoegi onions, chives, and spicy bean paste.

HAKATA

Hakata is a ward in Fukuoka City, and there's general consensus that Fukuoka is the birthplace of tonkotsu, the wildly popular, milky-white, savory pork broth. This broth is created by boiling pork bones over a long period of time. To preserve the milky-white color, the broth is usually seasoned with salt and/or miso. The noodles served are usually thin, firm, and straight. Typical toppings include chashu, wood ear mushrooms, scallions, and spicy mustard greens.

KYOTO

HAKATA

Seaside towns are more likely to use local fish and seafood in the broth and as toppings.

The cold north incorporates hearty miso into many of its broths.

SAPPORO

MURORAN

SAPPORO

This city is famous for being the birthplace of miso ramen. Hearty, rich, fatty, and delicious, Sapporo ramen is *kotteri*. A classic Sapporo miso ramen is a pork and red miso–based broth, with ground pork, garlic, ginger, and corn that's then topped with a dollop of butter. The noodles served in Sapporo are typically thick and chewy.

MURORAN

Muroran is a northern port city known for its pork curry ramen. In Japan, curry is often associated with sailors, and so Muroran combined its traditional curry with the emerging ramen trend in the first half of the twentieth century. The broth resembles more of a thick curry sauce than a thin soup.

TOKYO

Eastern Japan generally favors lighter broths (*assari*).

TOKYO

Tokyo-style ramen is typically a lighter broth (*assari*) most closely related to the original Chinese broth. Made with a hybrid of chicken and dashi fish stock with a soy sauce (*shoyu*) base, there are layers of flavor in this comforting dish. The style of noodle usually features medium-wide, curly noodles. Typical toppings include roast pork, scallions, and bamboo shoots.

UMAMI'S ROLE IN RAMEN

Umami is a Japanese word that translates roughly as "pleasant savory taste," and it is defined as the fifth taste or flavor. Umami has been described as a rich, meaty, savory taste that plays a significant role in making foods taste delicious and well-rounded.

THE HISTORY BEHIND UMAMI

The primary taste sensations—sweet, salty, sour, and bitter—are the base of flavor perceptions. Sweet and salty are easy to describe—think sugar and table salt. A good example of sour is lemon or lime. Bitter flavors include coffee, and beer. However, umami is trickier to pin down.

Umami has as much to do with mouth feel as with flavor; along with its rich meatiness, it gives the sensation of coating the tongue. It was first identified by Kikunae Ikeda in 1908 in kombu dashi. Around the same time, French chef Escoffier invented veal stock, which he found didn't fit in the four already existing taste sensations.

Asian cooking also relies heavily on balancing the four S's: sweet, salty, sour, and spicy. A perfect dish will be aesthetically pleasing and harmoniously flavored.

Explaining taste
Umami is not only the fifth taste, but has also been described as the perfect combination of the four tastes.

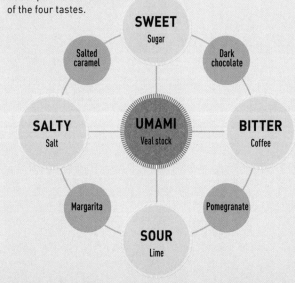

- SWEET — Sugar
- Salted caramel
- Dark chocolate
- SALTY — Salt
- UMAMI — Veal stock
- BITTER — Coffee
- Margarita
- Pomegranate
- SOUR — Lime

North America: Bacon
Bacon provides a smoky, salty, and even a bit sweet complement to dishes.

South America: Tomatoes
Raw or cooked, tomatoes provide a rich, sweet, and acidic flavor to dishes.

HOW RAMEN CAPTURES THE UMAMI FLAVOR

Umami may have gotten its name from Japan, but umami-rich foods have been eaten all over the world before the concept ever existed. Ramen combines umami-rich foods—whether Japanese, Western, or a mix of both—to create an especially flavorful, balanced dish.

In Japan, umami-rich foods include kombu bonito flakes, fermented fish, fermented bean paste, soy sauce, green tea, and shiitake mushrooms. Kombu dashi stock is a great example of combined umami ingredients that work really well together.

In Western cuisine, umami foods include ham, asparagus, and aged cheese. These flavors describe a shared taste of rich fullness and meatiness. Another example of umami is tomatoes, a fruit serving as the base of many sauces and condiments all over the world. The tomato miso ramen recipe is an example of a dish packed with Western umami-rich foods.

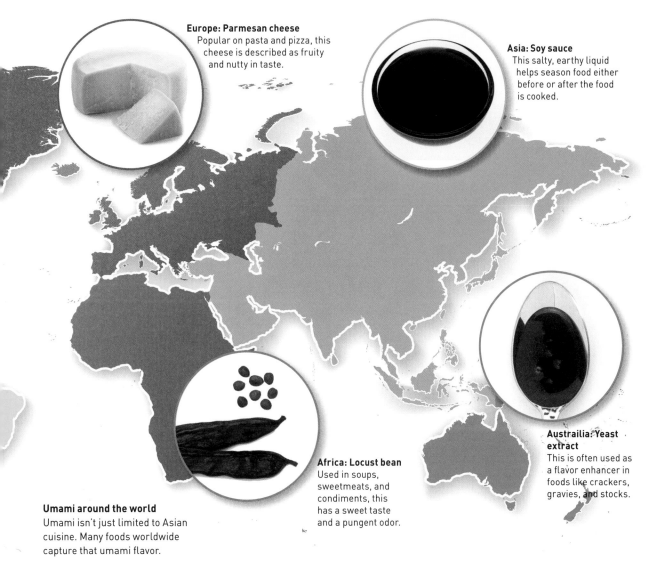

Europe: Parmesan cheese
Popular on pasta and pizza, this cheese is described as fruity and nutty in taste.

Asia: Soy sauce
This salty, earthy liquid helps season food either before or after the food is cooked.

Africa: Locust bean
Used in soups, sweetmeats, and condiments, this has a sweet taste and a pungent odor.

Austrailia: Yeast extract
This is often used as a flavor enhancer in foods like crackers, gravies, and stocks.

Umami around the world
Umami isn't just limited to Asian cuisine. Many foods worldwide capture that umami flavor.

WHAT iS FUSiON RAMEN?

In recent years, both Japanese and Western chefs have bucked tradition and created brash, bold takes on ramen. Chefs trained in the French tradition have contributed their knowledge of stocks to bring out as much flavor as possible in their broths.

TRADiTiONAL

From 1641 to 1943, Japan had a policy of isolationism that prohibited most contact with foreigners. It had only limited relations with the Netherlands, China, Korea, and the Ryukyu Islands. So up until World War II, Japanese cuisine had few outside influences. After the war, Japanese soldiers brought their favorite Chinese dishes, such as ramen, back to Japan and incorporated them into their own cuisine.

Flavors

Japanese cuisine has traditionally relied heavily on fish, rice, miso, noodles, and seasonal vegetables.

Ingredients

A typical ramen would be topped with items such as nori, soft eggs, menma, green onions, and pork.

Presentation

Ramen has traditionally been served in large, deep bowls. The noodles, broth, toppings, and flourishes are all layered in the same bowl and served piping hot to diners for greedy slurping.

Nori

Scallions

Corn

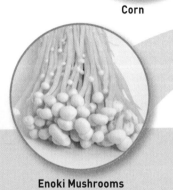

Enoki Mushrooms

FUSION

Modern chefs have taken ramen to exciting new heights by playing with various aspects of the dish, incorporating their own favorite ingredients and culinary techniques.

Blended cuisines

Fusion ramen can include components as varied as taco beef from Mexico, curry pastes from Thailand, and North African harissa. Using ingredients from anywhere around the world, you can play with your favorites while maintaining harmony with the flavors and textures as in traditional ramen.

Novelty

Traditional Japanese flavors can be enhanced by the introduction of food items that were only recently brought to Japan, such as tomatoes, Brussels sprouts, and coconut milk.

Unexpected techniques

Modern chefs have introduced techniques from traditional French cooking into ramen, including torching, sous vide, and foams. Transforming packet ramen noodles into a French-style gnocchi is just one of the ways chefs have incorporated fun techniques to modernize ramen.

Modern plating

Ramen has evolved from bowl service to being served in a variety of ways. For instance, tsukemen—otherwise known as dipping ramen—is a deconstructed ramen where the broth, noodles, and toppings are served to diners separately.

Tomatoes

Brussels Sprouts

Coconut Milk

Parmesan

KITCHEN EQUIPMENT

Having the proper kitchen equipment is very important in order to make the dishes in this book. However, don't feel you have to break the bank to stock up. Secondhand stores are a great place to source a lot of these items!

BOWLS

Mise en place bowls and plates Having multiple little bowls and plates to hold your prepared ingredients is the cleanest and most efficient way to set up your work station, allowing you to assemble your ramen bowl quickly.

Mixing bowls The two sizes of mixing bowls you need are a 4-cup (1l) mixing bowl for spices and smaller ingredients, and a 10-cup (2.5l) mixing bowl for larger ingredients.

CHOPPING AND CUTTING

Chef's knife Great for chopping, dicing, and slicing vegetables and meat. It usually has an 8- to 12-inch (20 to 30.5cm) blade and can come in a variety of sizes and weights. Simply choose a handle size and weight that's most comfortable for you.

Cutting boards These come in all shapes and sizes. I like to use plastic cutting boards for meat (as they are easy to clean and sanitize) and wooden cutting boards for preparing vegetables.

Paring knife This smallish knife with narrow-edge blade is perfect for more delicate kitchen work, such as peeling, skinning, and deveining your ingredients.

COOKING

Braising dish There are many different dishes that can be used to braise food—from casserole dishes, to cast-iron pots, to Dutch ovens. As long as your ingredients fit with the lid snugly on, you can use whichever dish you prefer.

Lidded stockpot Having a 12-quart (11.5l) or larger stockpot in your kitchen is very handy for making large quantities of ramen stocks. Look for a stockpot that comes with a heavy lid.

Noodle basket Allows you to cook and strain noodles, as well as blanch small batches of vegetables.

Pots and pans From heating broth to searing pork belly chashu, having a variety of durable pots and pans is necessary. It's best to find pots and pans with lids; however, if you don't have lids for all of them, you can always use aluminum foil.

ROLLING

Rolling pin There's no shortage of choices when it comes to a pin for rolling out your noodle dough. Options of wooden, marble, and plastic can be found in variety of shapes and sizes. Choose the rolling pin that feels the most comfortable for you.

Pasta roller and cutter An attachment can be fitted directly to a same-brand standing mixer. The roller and cutter roll out and portion the dough for noodles.

STRAINING

Skimmer This is used to skim the scum that rises to the surface of a simmering broth. Fine-mesh skimmers are the best for this.

Fine-mesh strainer This is great for pouring liquid through to catch any small bits you don't want.

Colander Needed to rinse and clean the bones in ramen stocks. Colanders have larger holes than strainers, allowing the debris from bones to be easily discarded.

UTENSILS

Ladle Great for portioning broth so you don't have to tilt a large pot. Choose a stainless-steel, sturdy ladle for ideal long-term use.

Slotted spoon Has holes or slots in the wide part of the spoon, allowing liquid to pass through while holding the food item. This is great for fishing out ingredients.

Tongs The ideal instrument for breaking up and portioning noodles, and for firmly grasping foods you're frying, grilling, or sautéing.

Rolling pin

An assortment of bowls

Noodle basket

Fine-mesh skimmer

Chef's knife

Cutting board

Fine-mesh strainer

SPOONS

Ramen spoons, also called Chinese duck spoons, are short-handled, large spoons with high edges, to maximize the amount of broth you can hold in them. You can find the spoons made out of wood, ceramic, metal, and plastic.

CHOPSTICKS

Chopsticks help you retrieve and eat the noodles and other solids from the ramen bowl. They're made from a number of materials and come in a variety of sizes. Choose the size and type of chopsticks you're most comfortable using.

SERVING UTENSILS

Only three main serving utensils are needed for a standard bowl of ramen: bowls, spoons, and chopsticks. For specialty ramen, however, you may need some other serving dishes.

For adding oils
or soy sauce

For serving toppings

For serving garnishes

BOWLS

Large, deep bowls are preferable for ramen, as you need a vessel big enough to hold the broth, noodles, and all of the toppings. Clay bowls work the best because they retain heat, but you can also use bowls made of ceramic or plastic.

SERVING DISHES

For specialty ramen such as tsukemen, or "dipping ramen," you'll need a variety of serving dishes to accommodate the broth, noodles, and toppings. You can use either a bamboo mat for the noodles, or any other vessel you have on hand, such as a plate or a bowl.

HOW TO EAT RAMEN

When it comes to eating ramen, you're expected to eat quickly, slurp loudly, and finish all the noodles and toppings in the bowl. In Japan, if you finish all the noodles in your bowl before finishing the rest of the dish, you can order another serving.

HOLDING THE UTENSILS PROPERLY

You need just two utensils to eat ramen: chopsticks and a deep spoon.

- Chopsticks are held in your right hand and used to grab the solids in the bowl, such as the noodles.
- The deep spoon is held in your left hand and used to sip the broth.

Intersperse eating the noodles and sipping the broth.

Digging in right away

If you order a bowl of ramen in Japan, it will arrive scalding hot. It's expected that you eat it as fast as possible to avoid allowing the noodles to become mushy. At home, in order to serve it as hot as possible, it's important to have all of the ingredients ready so you can assemble the bowl quickly.

Slurping the noodles

Slurping noodles cools them off just enough to avoid scalding your mouth, while keeping the broth nice and hot. This will ensure they don't become overcooked.

HOW TO USE CHOPSTICKS

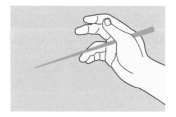

Rest one chopstick between the crook of your thumb and the top joint of your middle finger.

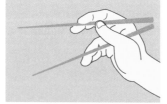

Place the other chopstick above it, holding it between your thumb and index finger.

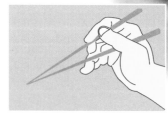

Practice moving the top chopstick up and down while keeping the lower one still.

GETTiNG TO THE BOTTOM OF RAMEN

Ramen, by definition, is a dish comprised of noodles, broth, and toppings. Understanding these components and how they work in harmony with each other is the first step in building the perfect bowl of ramen.

USING YOUR NOODLE

There's no standard ramen noodle. They can come in a variety of shapes and sizes, although most are made from high-gluten flour, salt, kansui water, and sometimes eggs. They are typically pale yellow in color, firm, and chewy. Different noodles are used for different broths, depending on what style of ramen it is.

FRESH, FROZEN, DRY, OR INSTANT?

Hardly anyone making ramen at home in Japan makes their own noodles, because good-quality, commercial ramen noodles are perfectly appropriate to use. While you can buy frozen noodles in some stores, buying fresh is preferable. Fresh noodles can be found in a number of Japanese and Asian grocery stores in the refrigerated section.

Instant ramen noodles are made by deep frying partially cooked noodles to dehydrate them into bricks. However, you can spend a bit more on instant noodles that have been partially cooked and air-dried, to avoid the deep-frying and the fat.

NARROW, WIDE, STRAIGHT, OR CURLY?

Oftentimes, you'll see thinner, straight ramen noodles paired with a tonkotsu broth, and curly with a miso-based broth. Wide noodles are usually paired with a flavorful broth to balance the natural taste of the noodle. If you're looking to get curly noodles, those are achieved with special equipment. Sun Noodle, based in three U.S. states, manufactures custom ramen noodles and gives an overview of the process on their website.

Fresh noodles
Comprised of strong flour, kansui, salt, and sometimes egg. Making your own fresh noodles is incredibly rewarding!

Dried noodles
Can come in a variety of shapes and sizes, and are versatile and delicious. Instant ramen is an example of a dried noodle.

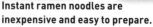
Instant ramen noodles are inexpensive and easy to prepare.

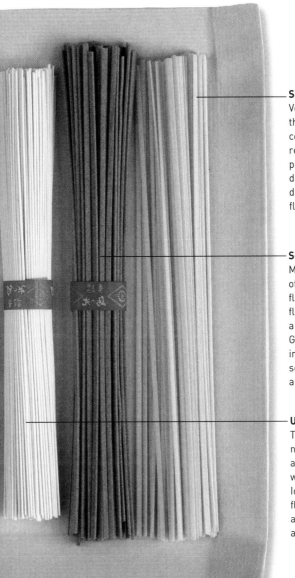

Somen noodles
Very thin, white noodles that are usually served cold. They're light and refreshing, making them perfect for a hot summer day. Usually found in light dishes with strong-flavored dipping sauces.

Soba noodles
Made from either a mix of wheat and buckwheat flours or just buckwheat flour, soba noodles have a slightly nutty flavor. Great as a cold salad, in stir-fries or hot soups, or chilled with a dipping sauce.

Udon noodles
Thick, white, wheat noodles that are soft and chewy in texture, with a neutral flavor. Ideal for stronger-flavored dishes, soups, and as a cold dish with a dipping sauce.

WHAT'S IN A NOODLE?

Two ingredients (or three, in the case of the egg noodle) play a vital role in ramen noodles. High-gluten flour provides the structure, kansui water lends to the texture of the noodle, and egg yolks help with the elasticity.

Flour

A wide variety of flours and starches are used in Asia for everything from thickening sauces to making noodles, pastries, buns, and tempura. In Japan, flours high in gluten are referred to as strong-strength flour, while flours low in gluten are referred to as weak-strength flour. For ramen noodles, high-gluten flour is used for a stronger noodle.

Kansui Water

Otherwise known as "lye water," kansui was traditionally found in well water used to make ramen noodles, but is now available in prepackaged bottles. Kansui gives the noodles their distinctive texture, bounce, flavor, and color, and is the key element that sets ramen noodles apart.

Kansui water contains sodium, potassium carbonate, and phosphate. It isn't always readily available outside of Japan, so instead, cooks use baked baking soda, which lends the same qualities to the noodles. The recipe for fresh ramen noodles given in this book uses baked baking soda instead of kansui water.

Eggs

Some ramen noodle recipes call for eggs, while some don't. Egg yolks are also sometimes added; I like the consistency and elasticity yolks lend to dough.

TAKING STOCK OF THE STOCK

Stock is the foundation of a bowl of ramen, lovingly transformed in a subsequent step into the broth that will cradle all other ramen ingredients. While stock used to be defined as bone-based, because of vegetarian stocks, it's now considered simply a prebroth, as it has not yet been seasoned. It's a blank slate, ready to be turned into broths by adding the appropriate seasonings.

INGREDIENTS

Many of the bone stocks require proteins for the body of the stock. These stocks also need kombu (sea kelp) and aromatics to impart flavor to them.

Proteins

Proteins in ramen stock include chicken and pork bones. When boiled or simmered for a long time, the collagen in the bones breaks down and gives the stock its viscosity (thickness). Protein in the form of meat in stock imparts flavor to the liquid. For instance, kombu dashi contains bonito flakes (dried, flaked skipjack tuna), which provides the lovely fragrant flavor in kombu dashi stock. There's also a certain amount of fat that's rendered in meat-based stocks. This rendering provides a boost in the flavor, as well as the texture, of the stock.

Dashi stock
Commonly referred to as kombu dashi, this light, fragrant stock is quick and easy to make. Dashi stock is a great base for many ramen dishes.

Chicken stock
This is a flavorful and comforting base for a variety of ramen dishes. Full of nutrients, it's very versatile and can be used for soups, sauces, and stews.

Kombu

Kombu, or sea kelp, is a sea vegetable often used for ramen. Kombu dashi stock, the simplest stock to make, only contains kombu and bonito flakes. Kombu dashi is only simmered for a short time in order to keep the delicate bonito from breaking down too much. Kombu is thought to be high in umami, and produces a lovely tealike flavor and consistency.

Aromatics

Aromatics used for ramen include carrots, garlic, onion, ginger, shallots, scallions, leeks, and apples. Variations of these ingredients are typically used for pork, chicken, and vegetarian stocks. The flavors of these ingredients impart different qualities to the ramen; for example, carrots have sweetness to them, while green apples provide sweet and sour notes, and ginger lends a spicy quality. Aromatics need to be simmered or boiled in liquid for enough time to infuse the liquid with flavor. Charring certain aromatics, such as onions, can give ramen a nice, smoky flavor.

STOCK PROFILES

Ramen stock is classified in a few different ways, one of which is heaviness versus lightness.

Kotteri

A kotteri stock is rich and thick. Tonkotsu is a perfect example of a kotteri stock.

Assari

These stocks are thin, light, and clear. A good example of an assari broth is kombu dashi.

Double stock

This refers to two different stocks being combined, such as chicken and pork. It allows for a more complex flavor and higher level of umami.

Pork stock
This stock gets its milky-white color from boiling bones for a long period of time. Making pork stock is a labor of love and requires time and patience.

Vegetarian stock
This is easy to make and is a great alternative to meat-based stocks. Flavorful, light, and refreshing, vegetable stocks can be made with a wide range of ingredients.

iT'S ALL ABOUT THE BROTH

Ramen broth is arguably the most important element of the dish. The process of converting a basic stock into a unique broth involves adding the appropriate seasoning and flavors for the broth you're trying to achieve. This process imbues the stock with different tastes, textures, and umami factors for each ramen recipe.

CREATiNG RAMEN BROTH

Tare

This is a seasoning liquid in which ingredients such as miso, soy, salt, and seaweed are mixed, boiled into a concentrated form, and then added to the bottom of a bowl of ramen. The stock is then added and mixed to form the broth. This allows for different flavor preferences based on the tare, not the stock.

Just as acceptable—and much easier for the home cook—is seasoning the broth directly before ladling it into bowls, which is the approach taken in this book. The benefit of not using tare is that you can season the broth precisely, and also fill the bowl with the noodles first.

Shio tare

Shio tare is the oldest and most traditional base for seasoning ramen. Shio translates to *salt*, and can refer to a wide variety of salts, as well as salt derived from the reduction of dashi or seaweed.

Miso

Miso is a complex fermented bean paste, and is considered the most recent ramen seasoning included in the three main categories (the other two being salt and soy sauce). Hearty and pungent, miso is a great base for kotteri broths.

Shoyu

Shoyu is a soy sauce–based seasoning. This can refer to a wide variety of pure soy sauces, or a more concentrated, boiled-down soy sauce. Shoyu tare is mainly used to season assari stocks.

SALT

Salt transforms a stock into a broth and is used in some form as seasoning in every broth, be it Japanese or French. From miso paste to soy sauce, all of the traditional ingredients used to season stocks to make them broths contain some level of salt.

VEGETABLES

There's no end of veggies that can be used in ramen broth. Mushrooms provide earthy flavors and great texture, while corn provides a lovely, sweet crunch. Bok choy, spinach, and other leafy greens are healthful additions to a dish, and make a beautiful presentation.

PROTEINS
Proteins added to the broth can be one of the main highlights of the dish. From rich bacon to light tofu, proteins alter and enhance the flavor, as well as provide contrasting texture to the dish.

FRUITS
Fruit is used consistently in the recipes throughout this book. Fruit can provide an extra layer of flavor and a touch of acidity that can highlight other flavors—for example, tomato can bring emphasis to the saltiness of miso.

ADDITIONAL AROMATICS
Using additional aromatics such as garlic, ginger, shallots, or carrots can enhance the broth and set the flavor profile of the dish.

BALANCING FLAVORS
The following are some broth-accompanying ingredients you can add based on the four S's of flavor: sweet, salty, sour, and spicy. However, some ingredients can span a couple categories. Pineapple juice, for example, brings both sweet and sour profiles.

SALTY
Miso (all types), dark soy sauce, white soy sauce, fish sauce, kelp

SWEET
Sugar, brown sugar, sake, mirin, tamarind concentrate, apples, tomatoes, pineapple juice

SOUR
Lime juice, vinegar, kimchi, tomatoes, pineapple juice

SPICY
Curry powder, harissa, Thai green curry paste, Thai red curry paste, chilies, chili black bean paste

FATS
The fats can give ramen added flavor, as well as body and a rich mouthfeel. Sesame oil is a great example of a fat that gives a broth tons of flavor while also building a bit of body. Tahini, coconut milk, peanut butter, and soy milk are also good additions to broth that contribute to the overall experience of eating a finished bowl of ramen.

TOPPINGS

Part of the appeal of ramen is the beauty of the presentation. The toppings are all neatly arranged and portray myriad colors, including golden yellow corn, dark green nori sheets, and white-and-pink narutomaki. Toppings can help create a well-balanced dish by adding texture and building on the all-important four S's of flavor (sweet, salty, sour, and spicy).

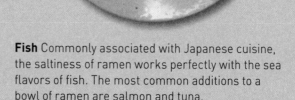

PROTEINS

Proteins are one of the main focal points in a bowl of ramen and provide a richness and meatiness that are in sharp contrast to the base of broth and noodles.

Bacon A wonderful addition to ramen, bacon's high umami content complements and perfectly adds to the flavor of the broth.

Cheese Many different types of cheese work with numerous ramen dishes. For instance, parmesan—which is high in umami—lends a rich, sharp flavor that can go really well with different types of ramen.

Chicken Known for its versatility, chicken can be prepared in myriad ways to give your ramen a flavor boost.

Chinese sausage A broad term for sausages made in China. They can be fresh or dried, lean or fatty. The most popular type is a thin, sweet, dried version. They can often be found in specialty supermarkets.

Duck Rich and full of taste, duck can nicely offset a lighter ramen broth.

Eggs Perhaps one of the most-loved ramen toppings, soft-boiled eggs—marinated or not—are a fabulous addition to a bowl of ramen. The soft egg yolk provides extra body to the broth, the marinated outer egg provides a tangy soy sauce flavor, and the white-and-yellow colors stand out in the presentation.

Fish Commonly associated with Japanese cuisine, the saltiness of ramen works perfectly with the sea flavors of fish. The most common additions to a bowl of ramen are salmon and tuna.

Narutomaki Also called *naruto*, this white fish cake has a red or pink spiral pattern in the center. The name stems from the spiral, which resembles the naturally occurring whirlpools in the Naruto Strait. The fish cake is a beautiful addition to a bowl of ramen. You can purchase long sticks of naruto and slice them in small rounds to garnish your ramen.

Chashu pork A common topping for ramen, chashu can be made from either pork belly or pork loin. The staple ingredients in chashu are soy sauce, sugar, sake, and mirin, although you can add other flavors.

Shellfish Many different types of shellfish can be added to ramen, from shrimp to scallops.

Tofu Made from soy, tofu has a spongy, cheeselike quality to it.

BALANCING TOPPINGS

As you know, Asian cooking seeks to balance those four S's of flavor. So while you can choose from many different proteins, fruits, or vegetables as toppings for your ramen, make sure you're putting together a balanced dish.

For instance, you don't want to use only ingredients that are salty to flavor your ramen. You also want to avoid using only ingredients with the same or similar textures or appearance. When topping a bowl of ramen, plan to incorporate a variety of colors, flavors, and textures. That way, you'll create a ramen that not only tastes great, but is also well balanced.

VEGETABLES AND FRUITS

Veggies and fruits are an important topping to ramen and can bring fresh flavors, various textures, beautiful color, and contrasting lightness to the dish.

Bok choy A type of Chinese cabbage, bok choy adds a pop of color and drama to a bowl of ramen.

Brussels sprouts Part of the emerging fusion ramen trend, which introduces exciting new toppings to the dish, the sharp taste of Brussels sprouts is a real winner when combined with more mellow flavors.

Corn The contrast between the sweetness of fresh corn and the saltiness of ramen broth is a perfect combination.

Fresh or pickled radishes With their strong, sweet flavor, radishes add a sharp tang to ramen.

Mushrooms Earthy, flavorful, and healthful, these are a common and excellent addition to ramen. For instance, shiitakes are known to be high on the umami scale and add a meaty texture.

Mustard greens When raw, mustard greens give a dish a spicy component. However, when cooked, they are mild and flavorful.

Pickled vegetables These add balance to a dish of ramen, offsetting the saltiness with sour.

Red bell peppers These peppers can lend a sweet, almost fruity taste to your ramen.

Spinach This can add a bit of bitterness and a delicate texture to a bowl of ramen.

Bean sprouts A traditional topping in Asian cuisine, bean sprouts are thin enough that they lightly cook when added in fresh to the broth, while still retaining a slight crunch.

Menma These fermented bamboo shoots have a mellow, woody flavor. They can be simmered in a variety of liquids for extra flavor and give a bowl of ramen a nice contrasting texture.

Apples From sweet to tart, apples lend a mild flavor along with a crunchy texture.

Tamarind Often used in Indian-style sauces or curries, this fruit provides great flavor and a sweet, pungent taste to ramen.

Tomatoes High on the umami scale, tomatoes can bring a rich, sweet, and acidic flavoring to a bowl of ramen.

FINAL FLOURISHES

You're almost ready to slurp down your ramen! But as a last touch, it's time to include a few enhancements to it. While they add visual appeal to the bowl, these do more than just garnish it; they add flavor and are definitely meant to be eaten.

BODY BUILDERS

Oils and fats can add flavor and richness to broth, and are often drizzled on top of a steaming bowl of ramen. Oils are a very popular condiment for ramen. Sesame oil, burnt garlic oil, and chili oil are a few of the most loved oils used to enhance flavor. However, use them in moderation, as many of them have a strong taste.

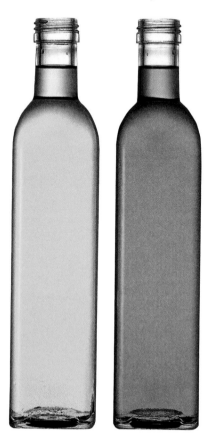

Burnt Garlic Oil
Burnt garlic oil, called *mayu* in Japan, balances rich dishes with a slightly bitter flavor.

Butter
A pat of butter is a common addition to ramen in various regions in Japan. Adding body and depth, butter goes well with miso-based ramen, as well as sweet corn ramen. For a dairy-free alternative, use a nut butter, such as peanut butter or cashew butter.

Chili Oil
Bright reddish-orange chili oil looks beautiful dotted in a bowl of ramen and provides a bit of heat.

Sesame Oil
Sesame oil lends a distinctive earthy flavor to ramen.

Different oils can add richness and body to ramen.

FINISHING SPRINKLES

There are many different finishing touches that can propel a good bowl of ramen into something really special. Nuts, flakes, citrus, seeds, and spice can all add oomph to a dish of ramen by providing texture and flavor.

Sesame Seeds
Sesame seeds provide a great texture contrast. Toasted sesame seeds bring a unique additional flavor to a bowl of ramen.

Cashews and Peanuts
Whole, chopped, or creamed, cashews and peanuts can make lovely additions to ramen.

Lime Wedges
Lime juice adds an acidic and sour profile, which helps bring out other flavors in a bowl of ramen.

Crushed Chili Flakes
These bring a level of heat to a bowl of ramen that can help balance the dish and add a level of complexity.

Bonito Flakes
Preserved and shaved dried skipjack tuna, these are used to make dashi stock, as well as for flavoring and garnish.

ASSEMBLING A BOWL OF RAMEN

Assembling a bowl of ramen should be done as rapidly as possible to retain heat and to keep the noodles from overcooking due to sitting in the broth too long. In order to quickly put together a bowl of ramen, all of the toppings and garnishes should be prepped, portioned, and temperature appropriate.

1 BOWL AND NOODLES

A ramen bowl should be deep and wide, in order to fill it with the noodles and broth and neatly display all of the toppings and garnishes. Clay bowls work the best, as they help retain heat well, followed by ceramic or plastic. There's no need to preheat the bowl, as long as your broth is piping hot.

A portion of uncooked noodles is 4 to 6 ounces (110 to 170g) per person. Cook the noodles minimally, according to the directions, so they retain their chewy, springy texture. Rinse the cooked noodles briefly under room-temperature water to eliminate any gumminess, and then divide them among the bowls.

2 BROTH

Some chefs fill the ramen bowl with a tare (seasoning liquid) and stock first, but other chefs season the entire stock prior to ladling it into the bowl. It's easier to adjust and control the seasoning by adding it to the broth first, so I've adopted this method for the book. You should just cover the noodles with the broth; this creates a platform for the toppings. After ladling the hot broth into the bowl, fluff the noodles slightly with a pair of tongs to ensure they aren't sticking together.

3 PROTEiN

It's important to neatly arrange the toppings to create a colorful and appealing display. The toppings should be arranged in differentiated sections, starting with the protein. If the broth just covers the noodles, the toppings should all sit nicely on top, without falling under the broth. If you're adding chashu pork, 2 to 3 slices are typically enough for a serving.

4 VEGETABLES

After arranging your protein, add the vegetables so they also sit in neat piles on top of the noodles. The vegetables used should complement the broth and the other ingredients. They should provide a contrasting texture, and a nice presentation.

You can use raw or cooked, in-season vegetables for your ramen. Sometimes, vegetables are even cooked in the broth, strained, and then added as a topping.

5 FiNAL FLOURiSHES

While there's no limit on what final flourishes you add, it's important to have a harmonious balance between what you choose. Scallions are a common final flourish for ramen. One tablespoon of scallions is a standard amount, but you can base the amount on personal preference. For a beautiful final touch, finish the bowl by tucking a sheet of nori halfway into the broth against the edge of the bowl.

PLANNiNG AHEAD

Making ramen can be time consuming due to all of the necessary components of the dish. Some of the components are best prepared the day before you're planning on serving ramen, so it's important to read through each recipe before you start in order to make sure you understand what to do and to allocate proper time for tackling it.

iTEMS TO HAVE READY BEFORE STARTiNG

The most important item to have ready before starting is the stock. Whether it's a quick stock or an all-day affair, the stock should be finished before you start on the ramen. Making a big batch of stock ahead of time and freezing it is an ideal way to ensure you always have backup and can quickly make a bowl of ramen. Also important to have ready beforehand are items such as chashu, which takes some time to prepare. Other items that you can make in advance include marinated soft-boiled eggs, menma, and noodles.

COOK AND PREP TiMES FOR COMPONENTS

This chart gives the approximate overall times for making all the basic recipes and stocks in this book. Make any of these components that your dish calls for in advance of making the dish itself.

Tonkotsu Pork Stock: 13 hours

Chashu Pork Belly: 12 hours

Chicken Stock: 6 hours

Marinated Soft-Boiled Eggs: 4 to 12 hours

Ramen Noodles: 3.5 hours

Chashu Pork Loin: 3 hours

Quick Pork Stock: 3 hours

Quick Chicken Stock: 2 hours

Secondary Dashi Stock: 1.5 hours

Vegetarian Stock: 1 to 9 hours

Menma: 40 minutes

Dashi Stock: 30 minutes

Soft-Boiled Eggs: 21 minutes

HOW TO PREPARE

After deciding which recipe to make, take note of the bolded items within the recipe ingredients list, which are the components you'll need to make first. The bolded items all have corresponding recipes within this book, so you have a basic understanding and step-by-step for how to prepare them. Make a list of the ingredients you'll need, for both the bolded items and the ramen recipe, and read through to make sure you have all the necessary kitchen equipment.

Once you're ready to begin the dish, make sure everything is chopped, prepped, and ready to go before beginning to cook. This will ensure the cooking and assembling process goes smoothly and quickly. You may need to plan a day ahead for some of the dishes, depending on what stock and toppings you choose.

THE CHEAT GUIDE!

• If you're short on time, the fastest recipes to make are the dashi- and vegetarian-based recipes, as those stocks are simple and quick.

• When it comes to the eggs, one technique for expediting the marinated eggs is to omit all marinating ingredients except for the soy sauce, and let the eggs sit for 15 to 20 minutes. With no water or other ingredients, the marinating process will take much less time.

• Noodles can be made in bulk and frozen—or just purchase them. You can also premake and freeze any of the stocks or chashu.

CHOOSING YOUR RAMEN

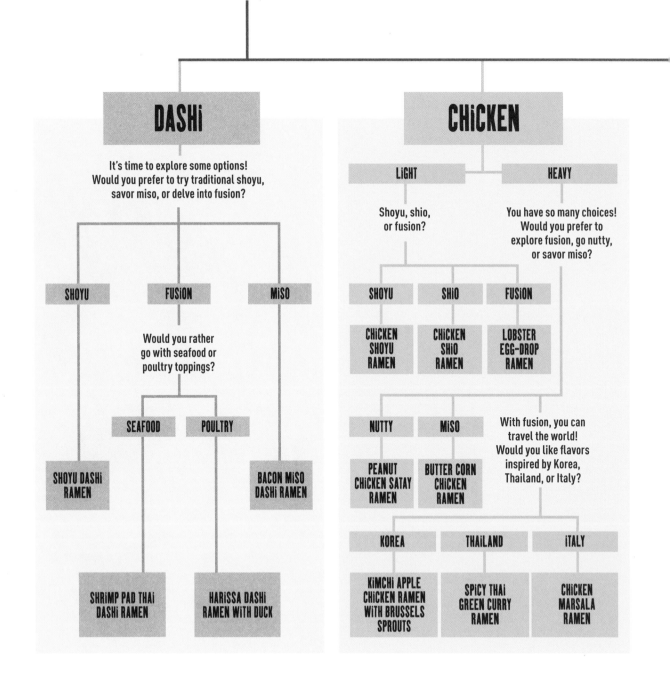

Having trouble deciding where to get started with ramen? Do you have a stock ready but no idea what dish you'd like to create with it? Simply answer the questions in this handy chart, and you'll be well on your way to finding the perfect ramen for you!

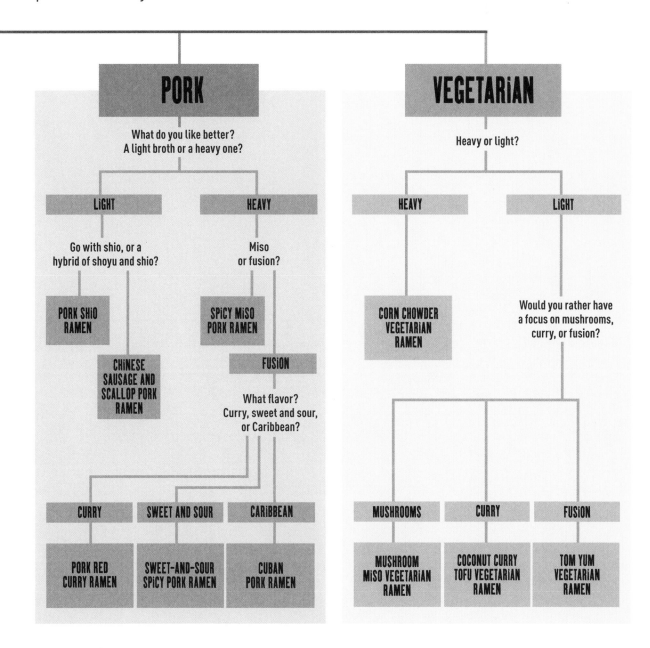

PORK

What do you like better?
A light broth or a heavy one?

LIGHT

Go with shio, or a hybrid of shoyu and shio?

PORK SHIO RAMEN

CHINESE SAUSAGE AND SCALLOP PORK RAMEN

HEAVY

Miso or fusion?

SPICY MISO PORK RAMEN

FUSION

What flavor? Curry, sweet and sour, or Caribbean?

CURRY

SWEET AND SOUR

CARIBBEAN

PORK RED CURRY RAMEN

SWEET-AND-SOUR SPICY PORK RAMEN

CUBAN PORK RAMEN

VEGETARIAN

Heavy or light?

HEAVY

CORN CHOWDER VEGETARIAN RAMEN

LIGHT

Would you rather have a focus on mushrooms, curry, or fusion?

MUSHROOMS

CURRY

FUSION

MUSHROOM MISO VEGETARIAN RAMEN

COCONUT CURRY TOFU VEGETARIAN RAMEN

TOM YUM VEGETARIAN RAMEN

BASIC RECIPES

Ramen, by definition, is broth, noodles, and toppings.
This chapter provides the building blocks for creating your
perfect ramen dish, with information on broths; recipes
for noodles, chashu, and menma; and ways to
prepare eggs and vegetables.

RAMEN NOODLES

Making your own noodles isn't as daunting as you might think! The main difference between regular noodles and ramen noodles is the presence of alkalinized water, which is known as kansui in Japan. You can either make your own kansui with baking soda as in this recipe, or buy a premade solution. To ensure accuracy when making these noodles, measure the noodle's dry ingredients in grams.

Prep time 2 hours **Cook time** 1.5 hours
Yield 4 6-oz. (170g) portions

Ingredients:
¼ cup baking soda
1 cup warm water
20g kosher salt
600g unbleached bread flour
4 egg yolks

Special Equipment:
Stand mixer with dough hook
Rolling pin
Dough roller and portioner

Baked
baking soda

Kosher
salt

Warm
water

1 To make baked baking soda, on a small sheet tray lined with parchment paper, spread baking soda in a thin layer. Bake at 275°F (140°C) for 1.5 hours. Let cool, and transfer to a sealable container. Be careful not to touch it when transferring to container, as it may irritate skin.

2 To make kansui, in a medium measuring cup, combine warm water, kosher salt, and 13g baked baking soda. Stir to dissolve.

Kansui: if you're using a premade kansui solution, substitute the baked baking soda in this recipe for 2 tablespoons of the solution.

3 In the mixing bowl of a stand mixer, place unbleached bread flour. Make a well in center of flour. Put egg yolks inside the well, and mix using a stand mixer on low for 2 minutes, until you see egg yolks distributed throughout flour.

4 Add kansui, and mix until flour starts to pull away from the sides of the bowl. (Mixture is relatively dry and can be difficult for a stand mixer engine.) Once fully incorporated, start kneading dough by hand in the bowl. Add more water if needed. Add 1 tablespoon water at a time—just enough to help dough stick together. Dough should come together without being moist to the touch.

Continued

5 Once dough is holding together, take it out of the bowl and knead it by hand on a flat surface until smooth, about 5 to 10 minutes. Wrap dough in plastic wrap, and let rest for at least 1 hour.

Storage: Wrap each noodle bundle in plastic wrap, place in a zipper-lock plastic bag, and refrigerate. Dough will last up to 1 week in the refrigerator and up to 1 month in the freezer.

6 Take dough out of the plastic wrap and roll it out using a rolling pin, until it is thin enough to be run through a dough roller.

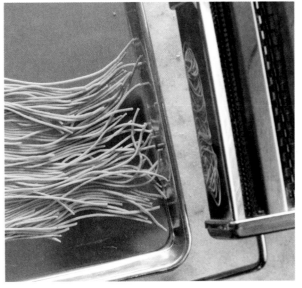

8 Run dough through a pasta cutter, at roughly ¼ inch (2mm) thickness.

7 Starting off slowly, run dough through the dough roller on each setting 3 times each, up until—and including—setting 4. At this point, especially if your dough is moist, leave it exposed on a table to dry out slightly before cutting it.

9 This gives you beautiful, straight noodles. (Curly noodles require special equipment.) Cut dough into roughly 14-inch (35cm) lengths of noodles.

COOKING FRESH RAMEN NOODLES

It's all about the noodles! The texture of the noodles in ramen dishes is very important. You can have a delicious broth, but if your noodles are soggy, it will ruin the dish. Cooked ramen noodles should be firm and chewy. Make sure your pot is large enough so the noodles are not overcrowded.

Prep time 5 mins   **Cook time** 2 mins   **Yield** 4 bowls

Ingredients:

24 oz. (680g) fresh **Ramen Noodles**

5 qt. (4.75l) tap water

Special Equipment:

Deep pot, 2 gal. (7.5l) or larger

Colander

4 deep serving bowls

1 In a 2-gallon (7.5l) or larger pot over medium-high heat, boil tap water. You should have at least 1 cup water for every 1 ounce (25g) noodles. Don't salt the water; the noodles themselves already contain salt, as will the ramen broth.

2 When water comes to a rolling boil, sprinkle Ramen Noodles into the pot, spreading them around with tongs to ensure they don't stick.

Cold-Dish Noodles: if you intend to use the noodles for a cold dish such as a tsukemen (dipping ramen) or noodle salad, rinse them under cold water immediately after straining to stop them from cooking any further.

3 Cook noodles for 50 seconds, stirring occasionally with the tongs to prevent the noodles from sticking to each other.

4 Turn off the burner, and drain noodles into a colander. Rinse them quickly under lukewarm water for 10 seconds, and then shake the colander to drain.

5 Using the tongs, divide noodles between 4 deep serving bowls.

CHASHU PORK LOIN

Packed with umami, thin strips of chashu pork loin are often saved for last when eating ramen, as if saving the best fireworks for the finale. Making chashu pork loin is simple and hugely rewarding, and the delicious broth can be saved and used for marinated eggs, seasoning (tare), reheating chashu slices, and garnishing.

Prep time 25 mins   **Cook time** 2.5 hours
Yield 2 pounds (1kg) pork loin

Storage: You can wrap any leftover unsliced chashu pork loin in plastic wrap and store it in the refrigerator for up to 1 week. Slice only as many pieces as you need at one time, and keep the rest in the refrigerator until you are ready to use it.

Ingredients:

2 lb. (1kg) pork loin

2 tsp. kosher salt

2 TB. vegetable oil

1 cup water

1 cup soy sauce

1 cup sake

1 cup mirin

½ cup dark brown sugar, tightly packed

5 cloves garlic, crushed

5 scallions, roughly chopped

1 2-in. (5cm) knob ginger, peeled and sliced

2 TB. lime juice

Special Equipment:

Butcher's twine

1 Lay pork loin on a cutting board. Roll and tie it into a log shape using butcher's twine, and rub with kosher salt.

2 In a large pan over high heat, heat vegetable oil. Add pork loin and sear on all sides, turning it with tongs, for about 10 minutes.

3 Add water, soy sauce, sake, mirin, dark brown sugar, garlic, scallions, ginger, and lime juice, and bring to a boil.

4 Reduce the heat to low. Cover the pan with tinfoil, pressing down to cover most of pork loin and liquid, but allowing some steam to escape. Simmer for 2 hours.

5 Remove pork loin, place on a cutting board, and allow to rest for 15 minutes. On medium heat, bring braising liquid up to a simmer, and reduce for approximately 5 to 8 minutes, until it thickens slightly and can lightly coat the back of a spoon. Remove from heat. Allow to cool before using it as a seasoning or marinade.

6 After meat has cooled, roll it tightly in plastic wrap to help it retain its shape and keep the moisture in. Store it in the refrigerator. When you're ready to use it, unwrap and slice it very thinly in rounds. That way, when you add it to broth, the liquid will heat it through.

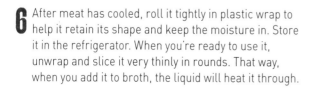

CHASHU PORK BELLY

Succulent slices of chashu pork belly are a welcome and delicious addition to most ramen dishes. Rich and hearty, with a high fat content, the pork belly is best seared before being added to the dish. One unique addition here is coconut milk, which marries well with the pork.

Prep time 8.5 hours   **Cook time** 3.5 hours
Yield 2 pounds (1kg) pork belly

Storage: Chashu pork belly will keep in the fridge for up to 1 week if placed in a zipper-lock plastic bag. it will also freeze well (for up to 6 months) if properly wrapped in a zipper-lock plastic freezer bag.

Ingredients:

2 lb. (1kg) slab pork belly, skin off

1 TB. kosher salt

1 TB. sesame oil

2 cups **Chicken Stock**

¼ cup white soy sauce

2 TB. sake

2 TB. mirin

1 TB. granulated sugar

5 cloves garlic, crushed

5 scallions, roughly chopped

1 2-in. (5cm) knob ginger, peeled and sliced

2 TB. lime juice

1 13.5-oz. (390ml) can coconut milk

Special Equipment:

Large ovenproof dish

1 Heat the oven to 300°F (150°C). Lay pork belly on a cutting board, and rub with kosher salt. If you have a large piece, you can roll and tie the belly into a log with butcher's twine.

2 In a large ovenproof dish, combine sesame oil, Chicken Stock, white soy sauce, sake, mirin, sugar, garlic, scallions, ginger, lime juice, and coconut milk. Transfer pork belly to the dish, fat side up.

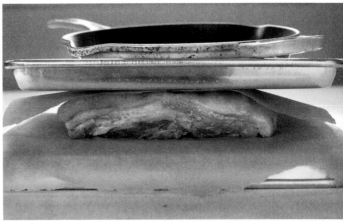

3 Cover the dish tightly with foil, and cook for 3.5 hours. Test for doneness by inserting a knife; meat should be tender enough to fall apart easily. Take pork belly out of the oven, and let it cool and rest for 1 hour to absorb juices.

4 Carefully transfer pork belly to a parchment-lined baking sheet. Place another piece of parchment on top, and then another baking sheet on that. Finally, place something heavy on top to weight it down. Transfer to the refrigerator. Strain pork belly juices and reserve for another use, such as seasoning your ramen.

5 Leave to sit overnight in the refrigerator. This will ensure pork belly is uniform and easy to slice. When you are ready to use it, place pork belly on a cutting board and slice it into 1-inch (2.5cm) thick pieces that are roughly 3 to 4 inches (7.5 cm to 10cm) long.

6 Before adding to your ramen, you will need to sear it to crisp it up and heat it through. Heat a nonstick or cast-iron pan on medium-high heat, and add a bit of vegetable oil. Sprinkle pork belly slices with a dash of salt, and add them to the pan. Sear until golden brown.

SOFT-BOiLED EGGS

Soft-boiled eggs, also known as 6-minute eggs, are a fantastic addition to ramen dishes. These eggs can either be used as is or marinated for extra flavor.

Prep time 15 mins   **Cook time** 6 mins   **Yield** 4 eggs

Storage: Eggs will keep in the refrigerator for up to 1 week. Before using the cooked eggs for ramen, let them come to room temperature, and then slice in half lengthwise.

Ingredients:
6 cups water
4 eggs

Special Equipment:
Ice bath
Timer

1 Fill a medium pot two-thirds full of water. Place over high heat, and bring water to a boil.

2 Prepare an ice bath for eggs. Fill a medium bowl with cold water and ½ cup ice.

3 Gently lower eggs into boiling water with a slotted spoon, and cook for exactly 6 minutes.

4 Turn off the heat, and immediately remove eggs with the slotted spoon to the ice bath. Let stand for at least 10 minutes.

5 Remove eggs from the ice bath, and carefully peel them. You may use them as is, or move on to the steps to make Marinated Soft-Boiled Eggs.

MARiNATED SOFT-BOiLED EGGS

These delicious eggs are a staple in ramen. The soft yolk adds body to the broth, and the marinated whites provide a great additional texture. You can add them to virtually any ramen dish!

Prep time 4 to 12 hours   **Yield** 4 eggs

Ingredients:

½ cup soy sauce

2 TB. sake

1 TB. granulated sugar

1 TB. cup mirin

1 cup water

4 **Soft-Boiled Eggs,** peeled

Special Equipment:

Medium zipper-lock plastic bag

Storage: Once eggs have been marinated, they will keep in the refrigerator for up to 1 week.

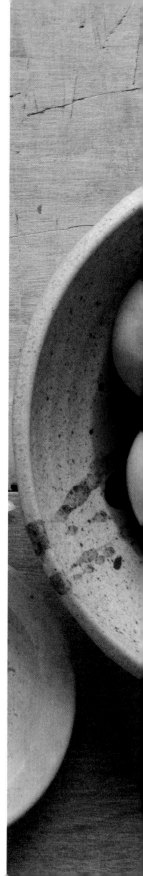

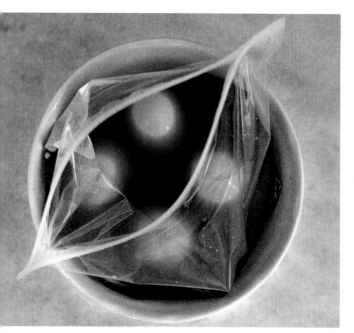

Prepare marinade by placing a medium zipper-lock plastic bag into a medium bowl and filling it with soy sauce, sake, sugar, mirin, and water. Stir to dissolve sugar. Add Soft-Boiled Eggs to marinade. Press the air out of the bag and seal. Refrigerate for at least 4 hours, but no more than 12 hours. Before using eggs for ramen, let them come to room temperature, and then slice in half lengthwise.

CUTTiNG SOFT-BOiLED EGGS

Cutting a soft boiled egg in half without making a mess of the yolk can sometimes prove to be a challenge. A cheese harp will provide the cleanest and easiest cut, but if you do not have one available you can use fishing line, unflavored dental floss, or a sharp knife.

Special Equipment:

A cheese harp, fishing line, unflavored dental floss, or a sharp knife

If you're using fishing line or dental floss, tie one end of the line to something and hold the other end very taut with one hand. Cup the egg lightly in your other hand; bring it up to the line, floss, or harp; and slice through.

If you're using a knife, place the egg on a cutting board. Start slowly with a slicing motion and then finish quickly.

MENMA

Menma is a condiment made from bamboo shoots. It's used in many different types of ramen and is considered a favorite topping for ramen in Japan. Although premade menma is available in Asian grocery stores, making your own is simple and rewarding.

Prep time 20 mins   **Cook time** 20 mins   **Yield** 2 cups

Ingredients:

1 garlic clove, minced

1 TB. sake

2 TB. soy sauce

¼ cup water

1 tsp. granulated sugar

1 tsp. rice wine vinegar

2 tsp. sesame oil

1 5-oz. (140g) can sliced bamboo shoots

Garlic

Granulated sugar

Sake

Sesame oil

Soy sauce

Bamboo shoots

Rice wine vinegar

1 Measure out all of your ingredients and mince garlic. In a small bowl, combine sake, soy sauce, water, sugar, and rice wine vinegar. Set aside.

Storage: You don't have to use menma right away. You can store it in the refrigerator for up to 1 week. Simply let the menma cool, and then place it in a plastic zipper-lock bag before putting it in the refrigerator.

2 In a sauté pan over medium heat, heat sesame oil. Add bamboo shoots, and fry for 1 minute. Reduce the heat, and add garlic. Add ingredients from the bowl.

3 Simmer for 15 minutes, stirring occasionally, until liquid has mostly evaporated. Transfer to a plate and allow to cool.

BURNT GARLIC OIL

Burnt garlic oil is a fantastic addition to a bowl of ramen. On its own, it can be a bit bitter, but lightly drizzled as a finishing touch, burnt garlic oil provides a deep, nutty flavor that creates a lovely contrast to a rich broth.

Prep time 10 mins   **Cook time** 20 mins   **Yield** ½ cup

Storage: For use at a later date, transfer burnt garlic oil to a sealable container and refrigerate for up to 2 months.

Ingredients:

¼ cup vegetable oil

10 cloves garlic, minced

¼ cup sesame oil

½ tsp. granulated sugar

½ tsp. kosher salt

Special Equipment:

Food processor or blender

1 In a small pot over medium-low heat, cook vegetable oil and garlic until it starts to brown.

2 Stirring constantly, reduce the heat to low and cook for 10 minutes.

3 Garlic should look dark and sticky. Once it does, turn off heat.

4 Add sesame oil, sugar, and kosher salt, and stir to combine.

5 Transfer mixture to a food processor or blender, and blend until fully incorporated, about 1 to 2 minutes. Oil is ready to use immediately.

PREPPiNG VEGETABLES

There's a saying that the sharper your knife, the less you cry. This means if your knife is dull, you risk cutting yourself when the blade slips on the skin of the object instead of slicing straight through. So it's important to have a very sharp chef's knife you're comfortable using. When using a cutting board, place a damp kitchen towel underneath to prevent it from moving.

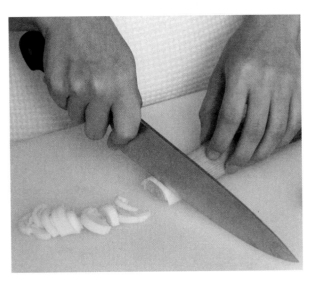

HOLDiNG THE KNiFE

In order to have complete control over the knife, move your dominant hand up the handle, so your thumb is on one side of the blade and your index finger is on the other side of the blade.

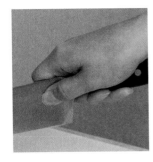

SLiCiNG

Gripping the knife properly, cut straight down on the vegetable, keeping your fingertips tucked out of the way of the blade.

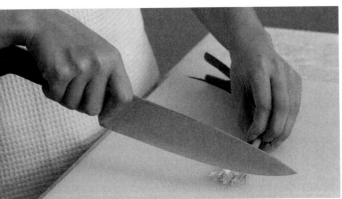

HOLDiNG THE VEGETABLE

With your nondominant hand, hold the vegetable you intend to cut in a clawlike grip, enabling the flat part of the knife to rest against your knuckles. This ensures your fingertips stay out of the way of the blade and avoid getting nicked.

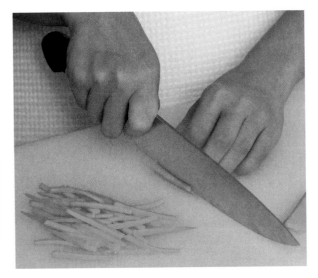

JULiENNiNG

Once you've cut slices, stack a few of them on top of each other and cut down at regular, short intervals to create thin strips.

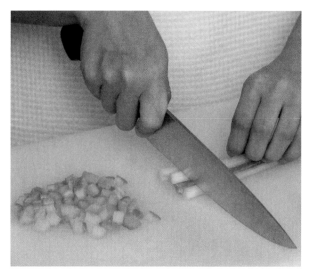

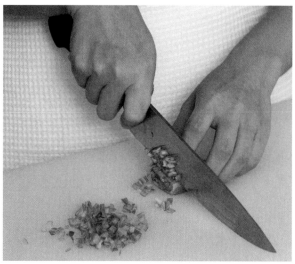

DICING

Gather julienned strips up and line them up perpendicular to the knife blade. Cut them into even segments to make cubes.

MINCING

After dicing, pass the knife repeatedly over whatever you're cutting, scraping up and flipping over the pieces to ensure evenness.

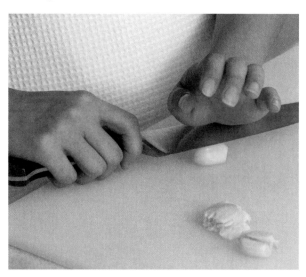

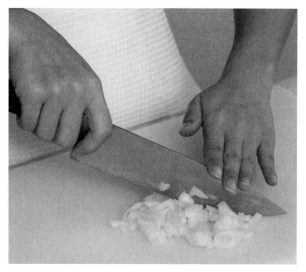

CRUSHING

To crush, lay the flat of the knife on the item, blade pointing away from you. With the heel of your other hand, whack the flat of the knife.

ROUGHLY CHOPPING

Hold the knife in your dominant hand and place the fingers of your other hand on the tip of the knife blade. Gently rock the knife back and forth.

RECiPES WiTH DASHi STOCK

Easy to make, dashi stock has a delicate, tealike quality that's incredibly versatile. Dashi's fresh sea flavors and subtle undertones pair well with ingredients such as fish, miso, and tofu.

DASHI STOCK

Dashi stock is present in much of Japanese cooking. A good dashi stock is actually incredibly easy to make. This particular one is a kombu dashi, made from kombu and bonito flakes. The flavor can be described as complex yet subtle and nuanced, almost like a fragrant tea.

Prep time 5 mins   **Cook time** 25 mins   **Yield** 8 cups

Ingredients:

5 6-in. (15.25cm) strips dried kombu

2 qt. (2l) water

1 cup packed bonito flakes

Special Equipment:

Fine-mesh strainer or cheesecloth

2 In a large pot over medium heat, simmer kombu in water for 15 to 20 minutes, making sure water doesn't boil.

1 Gently wipe kombu strips with a clean kitchen towel or a slightly moist paper towel to remove some of the residue, but not all of it, as it lends to the flavor.

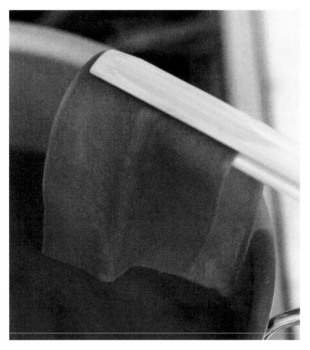

3 Leaving the burner on, remove kombu from water with tongs, and place into a large container. (Set aside for Secondary Dashi Stock, if you'd like.)

4 Add bonito flakes to kombu water, and gently simmer for 2 minutes.

5 Turn off the heat, and allow stock to steep for 5 minutes.

Continued →

6 Using a fine-mesh strainer or cheesecloth, strain liquid into a bowl. Stock should be pale in color and smell sweet and briny. (Keep strained bonito flakes for Secondary Dashi Stock, if you'd like.) Stock is now ready to be used immediately.

Storage: Cool the stock, transfer it to a sealable container, and refrigerate it for up to 4 days. You can also freeze this stock for up to 6 months.

Dashi Stock

SECONDARY DASHi STOCK

The previous recipe for dashi stock is honey colored, clear, and delicate, which is perfect for using in simple ramen dishes that don't have many additions, as the broth will stand on its own. This dashi stock will be slightly cloudy and can have a milder taste, making it good for miso-based soups, sauces, or simmered dishes.

Prep time 1 hour   **Cook time** 20 mins   **Yield** 4 cups

1 In a large pot over high heat, bring water, strained kombu strips and bonito flakes to a boil.

2 Lower the heat to a simmer. Allow to simmer for 10 minutes.

3 Turn off the heat, and stir in additional bonito flakes. Allow to steep for 1 hour.

4 Strain through a fine-mesh strainer or cheesecloth. Stock is now ready to be used immediately.

Ingredients:

4 cups water

Strained kombu strips and bonito flakes from **Dashi Stock**

$1/3$ cup packed bonito flakes

Special Equipment:

Fine-mesh strainer or cheesecloth

Storage: You can store this stock in the same way as the regular Dashi stock. if freezing, portion it in an ice-cube tray or into 1-cup servings first so you can easily use it.

Secondary **Dashi** Stock

SHOYU DASHI RAMEN

Dashi and shoyu (soy sauce) are a classic ramen combination, delicate and refreshing. This ramen is light but packed with a savory tang, which will have you polishing off every last drop in your bowl!

Prep time 20 mins   **Cook time** 20 mins   **Yield** 4 bowls

6 cups **Dashi Stock**

3 TB. soy sauce

¼ cup dry sake

1 TB. mirin

24 oz. (680g) fresh **Ramen Noodles**

8 slices **Chashu Pork Loin**, at room temperature

4 **Marinated Soft-Boiled Eggs**, sliced in half lengthwise

½ cup **Menma**

2 scallions, finely chopped

4 sheets nori

1 TB. shichimi togarashi powder

1 In a large pot over medium heat, bring Dashi Stock to a simmer.

2 Add soy sauce, dry sake, and mirin. Simmer for 5 minutes.

3 In a large pot of boiling water over high heat, cook Ramen Noodles for 50 seconds, stirring occasionally. Drain, rinse, and divide between 4 deep serving bowls.

4 Fill the bowls with hot broth, just covering noodles.

5 Neatly arrange Chashu Pork Loin, Marinated Soft-Boiled Eggs, Menma, and scallions on top of noodles in each bowl.

6 Tuck 1 nori sheet into broth against the side of each bowl. Sprinkle shichimi togarashi powder on eggs.

TSUKEMEN DASHI RAMEN WITH CHASHU

Tsukemen—dipping ramen—is a popular variation of ramen, one that's especially enjoyed during hot summer months. Dip the cold or room-temperature noodles into the broth, and soak up loads of flavor while staying refreshingly cool.

Prep time 10 mins   **Cook time** 10 mins
Yield 4 bowls

24 oz. (680g) fresh **Ramen Noodles**

3 cups **Dashi Stock**

1 cup mirin

1 cup soy sauce

2 TB. granulated sugar

4 scallions, finely chopped

2 TB. vegetable oil

1 tsp. kosher salt

12 slices **Chashu Pork Belly**

1 cup sliced shiitake mushrooms

4 **Marinated Soft-Boiled Eggs**, sliced in half lengthwise

½ cup **Menma**

Special Equipment:
8 serving dishes

1. In a large pot of boiling water over high heat, cook Ramen Noodles for 50 seconds, stirring occasionally. Drain, rinse, and divide between 4 serving dishes.

2. In a medium pot over medium heat, bring Dashi Stock to a simmer. Add mirin, soy sauce, sugar, and scallions. Reduce heat to low, and simmer for 5 minutes.

3. In a large sauté pan over medium-high heat, heat 1 tablespoon vegetable oil. Sprinkle kosher salt over Chashu Pork Belly.

4. Sear Chashu Pork Belly in the pan on both sides, about 2 minutes on each side. (Sear in batches, if necessary.) Remove from the pan and set aside.

5. In the same pan, add remaining 1 tablespoon vegetable oil. Add shiitake mushrooms, and sauté until golden, about 5 minutes.

6. Fill 4 bowls with warm broth. Divide cooked Chashu Pork Belly and mushrooms, Marinated Soft-Boiled Eggs, and Menma between 4 serving dishes.

7. Serve each guest a bowl of broth, a serving dish of noodles, and a serving dish of garnishes.

Serving Suggestion: You can serve the broth either cold or hot, and include garnishes in the broth, with the noodles, or separately. With chopsticks, dip the noodles into the broth, and slurp away!

TEMPURA SHRIMP DASHI RAMEN

The Japanese have been cooking tempura since the eighteenth century, after Portuguese missionaries introduced the technique. This dish is filled with a variety of great textures, including crunchy tempura shrimp, chewy noodles, and silky broth.

Prep time 35 mins   **Cook time** 25 mins   **Yield** 4 bowls

4 cups vegetable oil

6 cups **Dashi Stock**

⅔ cup soy sauce

½ cup mirin

2 TB. rice wine vinegar

2 TB. granulated sugar

1 cup all-purpose flour

¾ cup ice water

1 egg

12 large shrimp, peeled and deveined

¼ cup cornstarch

24 oz. (680g) fresh **Ramen Noodles**

2 scallions, thinly sliced

4 slices narutomaki (fish cakes)

½ cup cooked corn kernels

4 sheets nori

1 tsp. shichimi togarashi powder

Special Equipment:

Cooking thermometer

1. In a small deep pot, heat vegetable oil to 350°F (180°C) according to a thermometer.

2. In a large pot over medium heat, bring Dashi Stock to a simmer. Add soy sauce, mirin, rice wine vinegar, and sugar, and simmer for 5 minutes. Turn off the heat and set aside.

3. In a medium mixing bowl, sift all-purpose flour. Remove ice from ice water, put ice water into a small bowl, and vigorously whisk egg into it.

4. Pour egg mixture into the bowl of flour, and mix to just combine, being careful not to overmix.

5. Pat dry and lay flat shrimp. Sift cornstarch over both sides. Holding each shrimp by the tail, dip into egg-flour batter and then place into hot oil.

6. Fry shrimp until golden brown, about 3 minutes. Remove shrimp with tongs and place on a wire rack or a paper plate lined with paper towel.

7. In a large pot of boiling water over high heat, cook Ramen Noodles for 50 seconds. Drain, rinse, and divide between 4 deep serving bowls.

8. Reheat broth to a simmer. Fill the bowls with hot broth, just covering noodles. Arrange tempura shrimp, scallions, narutomaki, and corn on top of noodles in each bowl.

9. Tuck 1 nori sheet into the side of each bowl. Sprinkle shichimi togarashi powder over top.

SPICY MISO DASHI RAMEN WITH SALMON

Fresh salmon is not only extremely tasty, but is also a beautiful addition to a bowl of ramen. The dashi stock provides a great base for the salmon, while the fermented red miso paste perfectly complements the sea flavors of this ramen.

Prep time 20 mins   **Cook time** 30 mins
Yield 4 bowls

6 cups **Dashi Stock**

1 tsp. granulated sugar

¼ cup plus 2 TB. soy sauce

2 tsp. sesame oil

2 TB. rice wine vinegar

¼ cup red miso paste

2 TB. spicy fermented chili bean paste

2 6-oz. (170g) salmon fillets

2 TB. vegetable oil

24 oz. (680g) fresh **Ramen Noodles**

½ cup enoki mushrooms, trimmed

2 TB. white sesame seeds

4 **Marinated Soft-Boiled Eggs**, sliced in half lengthwise

2 scallions, finely chopped

2 tsp. chili oil

1 In a large pot over medium heat, bring Dashi Stock to a simmer.

2 Add sugar, ¼ cup soy sauce, sesame oil, rice wine vinegar, red miso paste, and chili bean paste. Simmer over low heat for 10 minutes.

3 While broth is simmering, pat dry salmon fillets and season with remaining 2 tablespoons soy sauce.

4 In a large sauté pan over medium-high heat, heat vegetable oil, and then add salmon fillets.

5 Cook salmon for 3 to 5 minutes per side, until cooked through. Remove salmon fillets from the pan and set aside.

6 In a large pot of boiling water over high heat, cook Ramen Noodles for 50 seconds, stirring occasionally. Drain, rinse, and divide between 4 deep serving bowls.

7 Fill the bowls with hot broth, just covering noodles. Break up salmon fillets into large chunks, and divide between the bowls.

8 Neatly arrange enoki mushrooms, white sesame seeds, Marinated Soft-Boiled Eggs, and scallions on top of noodles in each bowl. Sprinkle chili oil over broth.

CHOOSING FISH

Choosing fish can be a daunting process. Fresh or frozen? Grocery store or fish monger? Because choosing fish is just as important as how you'll cook it, follow these tips for choosing the right kind for your dish. Once you've selected your fish, be sure to handle and store it correctly to avoid spoilage.

FRESH FISH

If you are buying fresh fish, make sure it doesn't have any unpleasant odors. It should have a fresh sea smell. Beyond smell, there are some other considerations when making your purchase.

Once you've picked out your fish, cook or freeze it within 2 days of purchase. Fish should be stored in the refrigerator between 32°F and 41°F (0°C and 5°C) and in the freezer at 0°F (-18°C) or below for 1 to 3 months, depending on the type of fish.

When storing the fish, keep it tightly wrapped and in a zipper-lock plastic bag in the refrigerator.

Fins
The fins should be full, moist, and healthy looking. The fish shouldn't have torn or jagged fins.

Texture
The fish should be firm to the touch, moist, and a little slippery. When you press your finger into the fish, it should spring back immediately and not stay sunken.

Scales
If it's a scaly fish, the scales should lie flat and not be ruffled. The scales should be firmly attached to the skin and none should be missing.

Frozen Fish: Make sure they are thoroughly frozen. Avoid fish that have any signs of freezer burn or ice crystals, which occur when fish have been frozen, thawed, and refrozen. Defrost the fish in the refrigerator.

TSUKIJI MARKET

In operation since 1935, Tsukiji Market—located in central Tokyo—is Japan's largest and most famous seafood market. Each year, thousands of tourists flock to the market to witness the 2,000 tons of fish and seafood being bought and sold per day! The famous tuna auctions take place inside the market, while there's an outer market that houses stalls and restaurants. Over 400 different types of seafood product are sold at the market, as well as fruit, vegetables, meat, flowers, knives, and kitchen equipment.

The market is open from 5 A.M. until 2 P.M. The wholesale auctions are reserved solely for licensed buyers and run until 7 A.M., when the purchased fish is then moved for distribution nationally, or moved to the shops within the market for retail sale. Whole fish are then broken down with extremely large knives or band saws, in an awe-inspiring display.

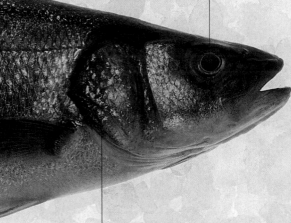

Eyes
The eyes should be shiny, clear, and bright. If the eyes are cloudy, the fish has begun to deteriorate. The eyes should not be sunken in.

Gills
Check the gills to ensure they are bright red and clean. Gills that are dark and slimy indicate the fish is no longer fresh.

The outer market caters to the public, with fish available to buy in small, non-wholesale-sized quantities.

MUSHROOM TOFU DASHI RAMEN

This healthful dish has a lovely earthy flavor, which is balanced with a bit of heat from the dried chilies. The dish can easily be made vegetarian by using vegetarian stock instead of dashi stock.

Prep time 20 mins   **Cook time** 40 mins   **Yield** 4 bowls

6 cups **Dashi Stock**

½ cup dried wood ear mushrooms

1 cup dried shiitake mushrooms

4 garlic cloves, crushed

8 scallions, finely chopped (reserve some green ends for garnish)

1½ tsp. crushed chili flakes

1 cup firm tofu, cubed

24 oz. (680g) fresh **Ramen Noodles**

1 cup fresh enoki mushrooms, trimmed

4 slices narutomaki (fish cake)

4 sheets nori, sliced into small strips

Special Equipment:

Fine-mesh strainer

Tongs or chopsticks

1 In a large pot over medium heat, bring Dashi Stock to a simmer.

2 Add dried wood ear mushrooms, dried shiitake mushrooms, garlic, and scallions, and simmer for 30 minutes.

3 Strain broth through a fine-mesh strainer, and with tongs or chopsticks, carefully remove dried mushrooms. Discard remaining solids, and pour broth back into the pot.

4 Slice shiitake mushrooms in half, and wood ear mushrooms into strips. Return to broth, and bring broth to a simmer.

5 Add crushed chili flakes and firm tofu. Simmer for 5 minutes.

6 In a large pot of boiling water over high heat, cook Ramen Noodles for 50 seconds, stirring occasionally. Drain, rinse, and divide between 4 deep serving bowls.

7 Fill the bowls with hot broth, just covering noodles. Add enoki mushrooms and narutomaki to each bowl, and sprinkle nori strips over top.

Straining Mushroom Grit: Dried mushrooms can be a bit gritty when rehydrated in the broth. Straining the broth after rehydrating the mushrooms can eliminate the grit from the broth while retaining the flavor.

SHRiMP PAD THAi DASHi RAMEN

A popular dish in Thailand—and one of my all-time favorite flavor combinations—the flavor profile of pad thai is citrusy, bold, and deep, which pairs perfectly with garlicky shrimp.

Prep time 20 mins   **Cook time** 20 mins   **Yield** 4 bowls

6 cups **Dashi Stock**

⅓ cup tamarind concentrate

2 TB. light brown sugar

1 cup soy sauce

3 TB. lime juice

1 TB. mirin

2 tsp. chili garlic sauce

4 scallions, finely chopped

3 TB. vegetable oil

1 TB. minced garlic

10 oz. (285g) medium-large shrimp, peeled and deveined

24 oz. (680g) fresh **Ramen Noodles**

1 cup bean sprouts, blanched

½ cup chopped peanuts or cashews

2 TB. chopped cilantro

4 lime wedges

1 In a large pot over medium heat, bring Dashi Stock to a simmer.

2 Add tamarind concentrate, light brown sugar, soy sauce, lime juice, mirin, chili garlic sauce, and ½ of scallions. Simmer for 10 minutes.

3 While broth is simmering, in a large sauté pan over medium heat, heat vegetable oil.

4 Add garlic and shrimp, and sauté for 4 to 5 minutes, until cooked through.

5 Remove shrimp from the pan with tongs and place on a plate.

6 In a large pot of boiling water over high heat, cook Ramen Noodles for 50 seconds, stirring occasionally. Drain, rinse, and divide between 4 deep serving bowls.

7 Fill the bowls with hot broth, just covering noodles.

8 Garnish each bowl with shrimp, remaining ½ of scallions, bean sprouts, chopped peanuts, and cilantro. Serve with lime wedges.

HARISSA DASHI RAMEN WITH DUCK

This North African–inspired dish contains harissa, a savory blend of red peppers, spices, herbs, and lemon—a perfect addition to a hot bowl of ramen. The duck is rich and full of flavor, providing a nice contrast to the light dashi stock.

Prep time 20 mins   **Cook time** 35 mins   **Yield** 4 bowls

6 cups **Dashi Stock**

6 TB. soy sauce

6 TB. prepared harissa

1 TB. granulated sugar

1 TB. rice wine vinegar

5 scallions, thinly sliced (reserve some for garnish)

1 cup shiitake mushrooms, sliced

2 6-oz. (170g) duck breasts, skin on

1 tsp kosher salt

½ tsp. ground black pepper

24 oz. (680g) fresh **Ramen Noodles**

4 **Marinated Soft-Boiled Eggs**, sliced in half lengthwise

2 TB. white sesame seeds

Scoring Duck Skin: When scoring duck skin, it's important to cut through the skin but not the meat. Scoring the skin will help to render the fat and crisp the skin nicely.

1 In a large pot over medium heat, bring Dashi Stock to a simmer. Add soy sauce, harissa, sugar, rice wine vinegar, scallions, and shiitake mushrooms. Simmer for 15 minutes.

2 Pat dry duck breasts with a paper towel. Score duck skin in a crisscross pattern. Season with kosher salt and black pepper.

3 In a medium pan over medium-high heat, add duck breasts, skin side down, and render fat for 7 to 8 minutes. Once duck skin is brown and crispy, turn breasts over and cook for 3 minutes.

4 Remove duck breasts from the pan and let them rest on a plate, skin side up, for 10 minutes. Reserve rendered duck fat to use as a garnish.

5 In a large pot of boiling water over high heat, cook Ramen Noodles for 50 seconds, stirring occasionally. Drain, rinse, and divide between 4 deep serving bowls.

6 Fill the bowls with hot broth, just covering noodles. Slice duck breasts on the bias, ¾ inch (2cm) thick. Divide duck into 4 portions and fan out slices on top of noodles.

7 Neatly arrange reserved scallions and Marinated Soft-Boiled Eggs in each bowl. Sprinkle white sesame seeds over duck. Drizzle 1½ teaspoons rendered duck fat over toppings of each bowl.

SOY MiLK DASHi RAMEN

This is one of my favorite ramen broths! This ramen is light, fragrant, and extremely satisfying. The soy milk adds a subtle creaminess and blends perfectly with the miso and ginger.

Prep time 15 mins **Cook time** 15 mins **Yield** 4 bowls

6 cups **Dashi Stock**

1 TB. minced ginger

3 TB. white miso paste

1 tsp. granulated sugar

3 TB. white soy sauce

¾ cup soy milk

1 tsp. kosher salt

24 oz. (680g) fresh **Ramen Noodles**

4 **Marinated Soft-Boiled Eggs**, sliced in half lengthwise

½ cup scallions, finely chopped

½ cup **Menma**

½ cup cooked corn kernels

4 small pats butter (about 2 TB.; optional)

4 sheets nori

2 TB. toasted sesame seeds

1 In a large pot over medium heat, bring Dashi Stock to a simmer.

2 Add ginger, white miso paste, sugar, white soy sauce, soy milk, and kosher salt. Simmer for 10 minutes.

3 Strain broth, making sure to discard the ginger afterward.

4 In a large pot of boiling water over high heat, cook Ramen Noodles for 50 seconds, stirring occasionally. Drain, rinse, and divide between 4 deep serving bowls.

5 Fill the bowls with hot broth, just covering noodles.

6 Neatly arrange Marinated Soft-Boiled Eggs, scallions, Menma, and corn on top of noodles in each bowl. Place 1 butter pat (if using) on each pile of corn.

7 Tuck 1 nori sheet into broth on the side of each bowl, leaving a corner sticking up. Sprinkle with toasted sesame seeds.

SHIO DASHI RAMEN WITH SEAFOOD

In this light, salt-based ramen, the fresh sea flavor of the dashi stock is a lovely base for the salmon and shrimp. However, feel free to use any seasonal fish or fresh seafood you have on hand.

Prep time 10 mins   **Cook time** 15 mins
Yield 4 bowls

6 cups **Dashi Stock**

2 TB. sake

1 TB. mirin

2 tsp. granulated sugar

1 tsp. white soy sauce

1 tsp. sesame oil

1½ tsp. sea salt

1 cup fresh shiitake mushrooms, sliced

8 to 12 medium-large shrimp, peeled and deveined

2 6-oz. (170g) salmon fillets, skinless and cut into 1-in. (2.5cm) chunks

1½ TB. fresh lemon juice

24 oz. (680g) fresh **Ramen Noodles**

½ cup scallions, thinly sliced

½ cup **Menma**

4 sheets nori

2 TB. toasted sesame seeds

1 In a large pot over medium heat, bring Dashi Stock to a simmer.

2 Add sake, mirin, sugar, white soy sauce, sesame oil, sea salt, and shiitake mushrooms. Simmer for 10 minutes.

3 Add shrimp, salmon fillets, and lemon juice, and simmer for a further 3 minutes.

4 In a large pot of boiling water over high heat, cook Ramen Noodles for 50 seconds, stirring occasionally. Drain, rinse, and divide between 4 deep serving bowls.

5 Fill the bowls with hot broth, just covering noodles.

6 Equally divide shrimp and salmon among the bowls. Arrange scallions and Menma on top of noodles in each bowl.

7 Tuck 1 nori sheet into broth against the side of each bowl. Sprinkle with toasted sesame seeds.

BACON MISO DASHI RAMEN

This dish is high on the umami scale! The combination of bacon and dashi is a heavenly marriage of flavors, and the miso and chili black bean paste bring depth and complexity to the dish.

Prep time 15 mins   **Cook time** 35 mins   **Yield** 4 bowls

3 strips smoky bacon

6 cups Dashi Stock

2 cloves garlic, crushed

1 ½-in. (1.25cm) knob ginger, roughly chopped

4 TB. white miso paste

1 TB. granulated sugar

1 TB. soy sauce

2 tsp. rice wine vinegar

1½ tsp. chili black bean paste

1 cup firm tofu, cubed

2 handfuls spinach

24 oz. (680g) fresh **Ramen Noodles**

4 **Marinated Soft-Boiled Eggs**, sliced in half lengthwise

2 scallions, finely chopped

1 Cut smoky bacon in 1-inch (2.5cm) pieces large enough to fish out of broth and to fry for garnish.

2 In a medium pot over medium heat, simmer Dashi Stock, garlic, ginger, and bacon for 20 minutes.

3 Strain broth while reserving pieces of bacon. Pat dry bacon with a paper towel.

4 Stir in white miso paste, sugar, soy sauce, rice wine vinegar, and chili black bean paste. Simmer for 5 minutes.

5 While broth is simmering, in a medium sauté pan over medium heat, fry bacon pieces until crispy. Set aside.

6 Add firm tofu and spinach to broth, and simmer for 5 minutes.

7 While broth is simmering, in a large pot of boiling water over high heat, cook Ramen Noodles for 50 seconds, stirring occasionally. Drain, rinse, and divide between 4 deep serving bowls.

8 Fill the bowls with hot broth, just covering noodles. Top noodles in each bowl with bacon pieces, Marinated Soft-Boiled Eggs, and scallions.

RECiPES WiTH CHiCKEN STOCK

Ramen dishes with a chicken stock base offer a nice medium body and light, clean chicken and vegetable flavors. From green curry, to marsala wine, to lobster egg-drop, you can make a variety of ramen fusion dishes with a chicken stock base.

CHICKEN STOCK

A very popular stock with cooks, chicken stock can be used for a huge variety of bases, from soups to sauces. One of the best things about making your own stock is you have complete control over every ingredient that goes into your pot, allowing you to avoid the sodium and preservatives with which canned chicken broth, base, and bouillon cubes are loaded.

Prep time 10 mins   **Cook time** 5.5 mins
Yield 3 quarts (3l)

Ingredients:

1 5-lb. (2.25kg) whole chicken

2 large carrots, roughly chopped (no need to peel)

½ cup garlic, crushed

2 bunches scallions (about 10 stems)

5 qt. (4.75l) water

1 yellow onion, sliced in half

1 3-in. (7.5cm) knob ginger, skin on

Special Equipment:

Fine-mesh skimmer

1 Place the chicken in a large stockpot on the stove. Add carrots, garlic, and scallions.

2 Add 4 quarts (4l) water to the stockpot, ensuring it covers the chicken with an excess of 2 inches (5cm) above chicken.

3 In a large cast-iron pan over high heat, char cut side of yellow onion and ginger until black and fragrant, and then add to the stockpot. You can do this in a dry pan, or over an open burner flame, by holding them over the flame with tongs or setting them on the grate. The aroma is absolutely heavenly!

4 Bring stock up to a boil, and then turn down the heat to a low simmer. Skim any dark foam and matter that floats to the surface with a skimmer for at least the first hour of cooking. During the entire process, chicken should be fully submerged in water, meaning you may have to periodically top it with the remaining 1 quart (1l) water. To retain clarity of stock, make sure it doesn't boil, but instead stays at a low simmer.

5 Once you have skimmed chicken stock periodically for the first hour, add scallions to the pot.

6 Cook, uncovered, for 2 hours. Carefully remove chicken, and allow it to cool slightly. Remove chicken meat, reserving for another use.

Continued →

7 Add chicken bones back to stock. Bring to a boil over high heat, and then reduce to a simmer on low. Cook for 3 hours, until stock has reduced to about 3 quarts (3l).

8 Strain stock and discard solid bits. Stock is now ready to be used immediately.

Storage: Cool stock, transfer to a sealable container, and store in the fridge for no more than 1 week. You can also freeze it for up to 6 months.

Chicken Stock

QUICK CHICKEN STOCK

If you're in a hurry and don't have the time to make chicken stock from scratch, cheat with this recipe.

Prep time 10 mins   **Cook time** 1.5 hours   **Yield** 7 to 8 cups

1 Add chicken breasts, carrot, garlic, yellow onion, ginger, scallions, and water to a medium-large pot. Bring to a boil over high heat.

2 Turn down the heat to medium-low, and simmer for 1.5 hours.

3 Strain stock through a colander, discarding any solids and saving chicken for another use.

Ingredients:

4 medium chicken breasts

1 large carrot, roughly chopped (no need to peel)

3 cloves garlic, crushed

½ yellow onion, roughly chopped

1 2-in. (5cm) knob ginger, skin on

3 scallions, finely chopped

8 cups water

Storage: The quick chicken stock can be stored in the same way as the regular chicken stock. For easy portions, divide stock amongst the wells in an ice-cube tray, or into 1-cup serving sizes, before freezing.

Quick **Chicken** Stock

THE DiFFERENT PARTS OF CHiCKEN FOR RAMEN

With its succulent, mild flesh that absorbs a variety of flavors, chicken is the most widely eaten meat in the world. One of the cheaper meats you can buy, chicken's not only useful in stock and broth, but also as a tasty topping for your bowl of ramen.

CHOOSiNG CHiCKEN

You can choose from a few different types of chicken to meet your needs.

- Young broilers or roasters have tender meat; older boiling fowl need to be stewed but have excellent flavor.
- Capons are castrated males that are fattened to produce especially tender, plump breasts.
- Free-range, corn-fed, and organic chickens are more expensive than intensively reared, but usually have better flavor and texture.

Drumstick
These make great finger food and are roasted or barbecued plain, marinated, or coated in sauce.

Leg Quarter
Comprising the whole leg plus a part of the backbone and sometimes half the tail, this cut has a moist texture.

Crown
A joint made up of two breasts attached to the breastbone, this is good for those who prefer just the white meat.

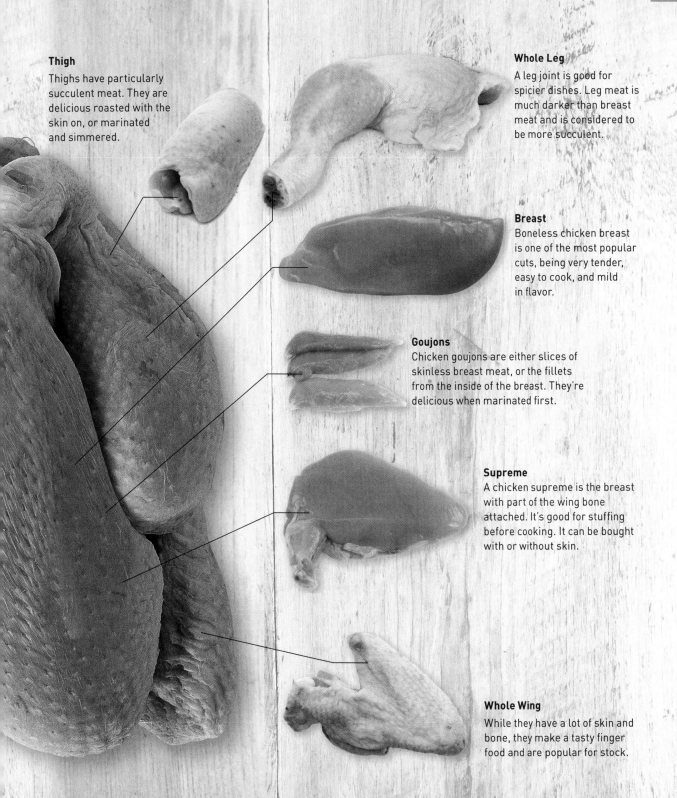

Thigh

Thighs have particularly
succulent meat. They are
delicious roasted with the
skin on, or marinated
and simmered.

Whole Leg

A leg joint is good for
spicier dishes. Leg meat is
much darker than breast
meat and is considered to
be more succulent.

Breast

Boneless chicken breast
is one of the most popular
cuts, being very tender,
easy to cook, and mild
in flavor.

Goujons

Chicken goujons are either slices of
skinless breast meat, or the fillets
from the inside of the breast. They're
delicious when marinated first.

Supreme

A chicken supreme is the breast
with part of the wing bone
attached. It's good for stuffing
before cooking. It can be bought
with or without skin.

Whole Wing

While they have a lot of skin and
bone, they make a tasty finger
food and are popular for stock.

CHiCKEN SHOYU RAMEN

I'm a huge fan of combining stocks, referred to as "double soups." Each stock brings something unique to the table, and by combining two or more, you can add layers of flavor. This light soy-based chicken broth is subtle and nuanced; adding dashi gives the ramen a sea-fresh flavor.

Prep time 20 mins   **Cook time** 20 mins   **Yield** 4 bowls

4 cups **Chicken Stock**

2 cups **Dashi Stock**

1 2-in. (5cm) knob ginger, sliced and skin on

4 cloves garlic, crushed

¼ cup plus 1 TB. soy sauce

3 TB. sake

2 TB. mirin

1½ tsp. granulated sugar

24 oz. (680g) fresh **Ramen Noodles**

2 cups chicken, cooked and shredded

¼ cup scallions

4 **Marinated Soft-Boiled Eggs**, sliced

1 In a large pot over medium heat, bring Chicken Stock and Dashi Stock to a simmer.

2 Add ginger, garlic, soy sauce, sake, mirin, and sugar. Simmer for 15 minutes. Strain broth, discarding any solids.

3 In a large pot of boiling water over high heat, cook Ramen Noodles for 50 seconds, stirring occasionally. Drain, rinse, and divide between 4 deep serving bowls.

4 Fill the bowls with hot broth, just covering noodles.

5 Neatly arrange shredded chicken, scallions, and Marinated Soft-Boiled Eggs on top of noodles in each bowl.

GINGER CHICKEN RAMEN

Just like homemade chicken soup, a bowl of chicken ramen is the ultimate comfort food. Spicy ginger is a prominent flavor in this dish, enhanced by the subtle white soy sauce. Flavorful, filling, and nourishing, this dish will please the entire family.

Prep time 20 mins **Cook time** 45 mins **Yield** 4 bowls

4 cups **Chicken Stock**

2 cups **Quick Pork Stock**

2 medium boneless, skinless chicken breasts

1 TB. minced ginger

2 tsp. minced garlic

1/3 cup white soy sauce

3 TB. mirin

1 tsp. granulated sugar

1 tsp. sesame oil

2 tsp. kosher salt (optional)

24 oz. (680g) fresh **Ramen Noodles**

1/4 cup scallions

4 **Marinated Soft-Boiled Eggs**, sliced in half lengthwise

4 sheets nori

1/4 cup sesame seeds

1 In a large pot over medium heat, bring Chicken Stock and Quick Pork Stock to a simmer.

2 Add chicken breasts, ginger, garlic, white soy sauce, mirin, sugar, and sesame oil. Simmer for 30 to 40 minutes, until chicken is cooked through.

3 Remove chicken and let cool slightly before slicing. Set aside.

4 Taste broth and season with kosher salt (if using). Turn off heat until just before noodles are done, and then reheat.

5 In a large pot of boiling water over high heat, cook Ramen Noodles for 50 seconds, stirring occasionally. Drain, rinse, and divide between 4 deep serving bowls.

6 Fill the bowls with hot broth, just covering noodles.

7 Neatly arrange sliced chicken, scallions, and Marinated Soft-Boiled Eggs on top of noodles in each bowl.

8 Tuck 1 nori sheet into broth against the side of each bowl. Sprinkle with sesame seeds.

DOUBLE MiSO RAMEN

The salty, fermented complexity of miso makes it a popular seasoning ingredient in Japan. As well as providing a wide variety of health benefits, miso gives depth of flavor to ramen. The addition of dashi stock provides another layer of flavor to this dish.

Prep time 10 mins　**Cook time** 10 mins　**Yield** 4 bowls

4 cups **Chicken Stock**

2 cups **Dashi Stock**

1 tsp. granulated sugar

1 TB. soy sauce

3 TB. white miso paste

½ tsp. sesame oil

1 cup firm tofu, cubed

24 oz. (680g) fresh **Ramen Noodles**

½ cup enoki mushrooms

2 scallions, thinly sliced

1 cup fresh bean sprouts, blanched

4 **Marinated Soft-Boiled Eggs**, sliced in half lengthwise

1 In a large pot over medium heat, bring Chicken Stock and Dashi Stock to a simmer.

2 Add sugar, soy sauce, white miso paste, sesame oil, and firm tofu. Simmer for 5 minutes.

3 In a large pot of boiling water over high heat, cook Ramen Noodles for 50 seconds, stirring occasionally. Drain, rinse, and divide between 4 deep serving bowls.

4 Fill the bowls with hot broth, just covering noodles.

5 Neatly arrange enoki mushrooms, scallions, bean sprouts, and Marinated Soft-Boiled Eggs on top of noodles in each bowl.

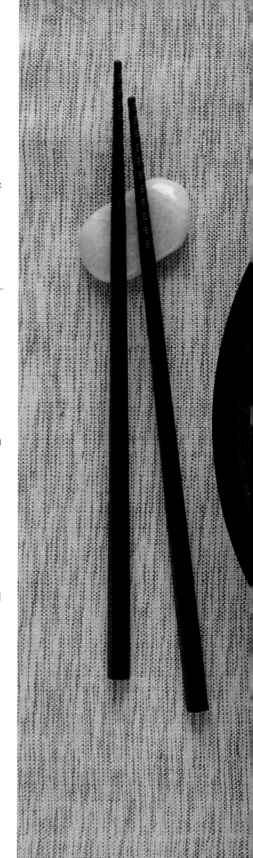

TANTANMEN CHiCKEN RAMEN

Packed with heat, this dish features sesame and chili as the predominant flavors. The pickled vegetables balance the dish with a nice touch of sour.

Prep time 10 mins   **Cook time** 20 mins   **Yield** 4 bowls

6 cups **Chicken Stock**

2 tsp. minced ginger

2 tsp. minced garlic

1 TB. soy sauce

1 TB. granulated sugar

2 TB. neri goma or tahini sesame paste

2 TB. chili garlic sauce

24 oz. (680g) fresh **Ramen Noodles**

1 cup pickled vegetables

8 thin slices **Chashu Pork Loin**, at room temperature

½ cup scallions, finely chopped

1 tsp. sesame oil

1 In a large pot over medium heat, bring Chicken Stock, ginger, garlic, soy sauce, sugar, neri goma, and chili garlic sauce to a simmer.

2 Simmer broth for 15 minutes, stirring occasionally.

3 In a large pot of boiling water over high heat, cook Ramen Noodles for 50 seconds, stirring occasionally. Drain, rinse, and divide between 4 deep serving bowls.

4 Fill the bowls with hot broth, just covering noodles.

5 Neatly arrange pickled vegetables, Chashu Pork Loin, and scallions on top of noodles in each bowl. Sprinkle with sesame oil.

KiMCHi APPLE CHiCKEN RAMEN WiTH BRUSSELS SPROUTS

Pan-fried Brussels sprouts taste fantastic in ramen and are the stars of this dish. The combination of soy and kimchi with the sprouts—along with the more mellow flavors of apple and miso for balance—is definitely a winner!

Prep time 20 mins **Cook time** 30 mins **Yield** 4 bowls

4 cups **Chicken Stock**

2 cups **Quick Pork Stock**

¾ cup kimchi

1 Granny Smith apple, cored, peeled, and diced

1 TB. white miso paste

2 TB. soy sauce

2 tsp. granulated sugar

2 TB. vegetable oil

2 cups Brussels sprouts, trimmed and sliced in half

1 TB. minced garlic

2 TB. reduced-sodium soy sauce

24 oz. (680g) fresh **Ramen Noodles**

1 In a large pot over medium heat, bring Chicken Stock and Quick Pork Stock to a simmer.

2 Add kimchi, Granny Smith apple, white miso paste, soy sauce, and sugar. Simmer for 15 minutes.

3 While broth is simmering, in a large pan over medium-high heat, heat vegetable oil. Add Brussels sprouts and garlic to the pan, and cook for 10 minutes, stirring frequently.

4 Add reduced-sodium soy sauce to sprouts, and cook for 2 more minutes. Turn off the heat and set aside.

5 In a large pot of boiling water over high heat, cook Ramen Noodles for 50 seconds, stirring occasionally. Drain, rinse, and divide between 4 deep serving bowls.

6 Fill the bowls with hot broth, just covering noodles. Arrange Brussels sprouts in the middle of each bowl.

SARATANMEN CHiCKEN RAMEN

This sweet-and-sour broth is the perfect way to warm up on a cold day. Originating in China, this dish has a touch of black vinegar, which gives it a unique fruity flavor.

Prep time 25 mins   **Cook time** 30 mins   **Yield** 4 bowls

---

6 cups **Chicken Stock**

¾ cup carrot, roughly chopped

½ white onion, roughly chopped

1 2-in. (5cm) knob ginger, peeled and sliced

4 shiitake mushrooms, sliced in half

2 TB. soy sauce

4 TB. black vinegar

1 TB. sake

1 tsp. granulated sugar

1 tsp. kosher salt

¾ cup pineapple juice

2 tsp. chili paste

24 oz. (680g) fresh **Ramen Noodles**

1 cup chicken, cooked and shredded

¼ cup bamboo shoots

2 TB. cilantro, chopped

1 In a large pot over medium heat, bring Chicken Stock to a simmer.

2 Add carrot, white onion, ginger, and shiitake mushrooms, and simmer for 20 minutes.

3 Add soy sauce, black vinegar, sake, sugar, kosher salt, and pineapple juice. Simmer for 5 minutes. Taste and adjust seasonings as needed.

4 Strain broth, reserving only shiitake mushrooms for garnishing. Discard remaining ingredients.

5 Bring broth back up to a simmer over medium heat. Add chili paste.

6 In a large pot of boiling water over high heat, cook Ramen Noodles for 50 seconds, stirring occasionally. Drain, rinse, and divide between 4 deep serving bowls.

7 Fill the bowls with hot broth, just covering noodles.

8 Garnish each bowl with chicken, reserved shiitake mushrooms, bamboo shoots, and cilantro.

MAZEMEN RAMEN WITH TUNA

Mazemen ramen is served with very little broth, converting it to a "dry" style of ramen that showcases the toppings. With so little liquid in the dish, the broth needs to be bold and packed with flavor. The fresh ahi tuna steals the show in this dish, providing great texture and picking up flavors from the broth.

Prep time 15 mins **Cook time** 20 mins **Yield** 4 bowls

10 oz. (285g) fresh ahi tuna, wrapped in plastic wrap and frozen for just 1 hour

1 cup **Chicken Stock**

¾ cup **Quick Pork Stock**

1 tsp. minced fresh ginger

1 tsp. minced garlic

1 TB. sake

2 TB. soy sauce

24 oz. (680g) fresh **Ramen Noodles**

4 **Marinated Soft-Boiled Eggs**

1 cup cooked corn kernels

2 scallions, finely chopped

2 TB. sesame seeds

¼ cup nori, finely sliced into ribbons

1 TB. bonito flakes

1 Remove ahi tuna from the freezer, take off plastic wrap, and cube with a very sharp knife.

2 In a large pot over medium heat, bring Chicken Stock and Quick Pork Stock to a simmer.

3 Add ginger, garlic, sake, and soy sauce. Simmer for 15 minutes.

4 In a large pot of boiling water over high heat, cook Ramen Noodles for 50 seconds, stirring occasionally. Drain, rinse, and divide between 4 deep serving bowls.

5 Divide hot broth between the bowls. Broth won't cover noodles.

6 Neatly arrange Marinated Soft-Boiled Eggs, corn, ahi tuna, and scallions on top of noodles in each bowl. Sprinkle with sesame seeds, nori, and bonito flakes.

Cooked Tuna: Ahi tuna is sushi grade and can be eaten raw. if you prefer to cook your tuna, however, you can season it and then sear it in a hot pan with vegetable oil.

SPICY THAI GREEN CURRY RAMEN

This dish combines two of my favorite foods: ramen and green curry. The green curry paste is a delightful blend of green chilies, galangal, garlic, lemongrass, shrimp paste, lime, cilantro, and spices. Fragrant and spicy, the recipe is mellowed with a touch of creamy coconut milk. Get ready to be transported to Asia!

Prep time 20 mins   **Cook time** 30 mins   **Yield** 4 bowls

2 medium boneless, skinless chicken breasts

6 cups **Chicken Stock**

1 TB. green curry paste

2 TB. soy sauce

1½ cups fresh oyster or shiitake mushrooms, sliced

2 to 3 small Thai bird's-eye chilies, finely chopped

2 tsp. granulated sugar

¾ cup coconut milk

½ cup firm tofu, cubed

1 TB. fresh lime juice

24 oz. (680g) fresh **Ramen Noodles**

2 TB. cilantro, finely chopped

1 Rinse chicken breasts under cold water, pat dry, and cut into 1-inch (2.5cm) cubes. Set aside.

2 In a large pot over medium heat, bring Chicken Stock to a simmer.

3 Add chicken cubes, green curry paste, soy sauce, oyster mushrooms, Thai bird's-eye chilies, and sugar. Simmer for 20 minutes.

4 Add coconut milk, firm tofu, and lime juice, and simmer for a further 5 minutes.

5 In a large pot of boiling water over high heat, cook Ramen Noodles for 50 seconds, stirring occasionally. Drain, rinse, and divide between 4 deep serving bowls.

6 Fill the bowls with hot broth, just covering noodles.

7 Scoop out equal portions of chicken into each bowl. Sprinkle cilantro over each bowl.

LOBSTER EGG-DROP RAMEN

This simple Chinese-inspired broth, similar to traditional egg-drop soup, is elevated to gourmet ramen status with the addition of lobster.

Prep time 15 mins   **Cook time** 20 mins
Yield 4 bowls

6 cups **Chicken Stock**

1 tsp. minced fresh ginger

1 tsp. minced garlic

1 TB. sake

6 scallions, finely chopped (reserve some green ends for garnish)

1 TB. fish sauce or white soy sauce

2 tsp. kosher salt

2 5-oz. (140g) lobster tails

2 eggs

2 TB. cornstarch mixed with ½ cup cold water

24 oz. (680g) fresh **Ramen Noodles**

1 cup cooked corn kernels

4 sheets nori

Special Equipment:

Ice bath

1 In a large pot over medium heat, bring Chicken Stock to a simmer.

2 Add ginger, garlic, sake, scallions, fish sauce, and kosher salt. Simmer for 5 minutes. Add lobster tails, and simmer for 5 minutes.

3 While broth is simmering, in a medium bowl, whisk eggs. Set aside.

4 Remove lobster tails from broth, and drop into an ice bath. While lobster is chilling, add cornstarch mixture to broth.

5 Bring broth up to a boil, stir, and drizzle in egg mixture a bit at a time; mixture will cook immediately. Turn down the heat to low.

6 Remove meat from lobster tails, cut in large chunks, and return to broth.

7 In a large pot of boiling water over high heat, cook Ramen Noodles for 50 seconds, stirring occasionally. Drain, rinse, and divide between 4 deep serving bowls.

8 Fill the bowls with hot broth, just covering noodles.

9 Equally distribute lobster meat and corn between the bowls. Tuck 1 nori sheet into broth against the side of each bowl.

HOW TO PREPARE LOBSTER

Are you new to cooking lobster? Do you simply have trouble getting all the meat out of it? Never fear! Removing lobster meat is a quick and easy process. Soon enough, you'll have all your yummy lobster meat ready to add to your ramen.

WHOLE LOBSTER

Lobsters are available to buy both live and already prepared. If you'd prefer not to take a live lobster home, the store will often prepare it for you, but be sure to pick the meat out of the shell that day. When choosing a live lobster, pick one that is lively. It should move its claws and even flap its tail. Limp lobsters should be avoided.

Claw

Tail

Shell

Mandible

PREPARING LOBSTER TAIL

1 Take firm hold of the tail section and twist sharply to separate it from the body and head section.

2 Turn the lobster tail over, so the underside is face up. Using kitchen scissors, cut down the center of the shell.

FROZEN LOBSTER TAIL CAUTIONS

When picking out frozen lobster tail for your ramen, you want the freshest and best-quality tails you can find. The following are some common issues to watch out for:

- If possible, choose cold-water tails over warm-water tails. Warm-water tails are more likely to have issues with quality.
- Any lobster tails at deep discount are most likely warm-water tails and therefore lower in quality. Basically, you get what you pay for.
- Discoloration in the flesh, especially black spots, indicates the tails were not handled properly.
- Tails with a grayish color signify the lobster wasn't alive during processing.
- The meat shouldn't be dull or yellow. Look for white meat.
- Watch for glazing, a process in which water is injected between the meat and the shell before freezing. This can add weight to the tails and lead to higher pricing for less meat.

PREPARING LOBSTER CLAWS

1 With a lobster cracker or a small hammer, crack open the claw shells. Take care not to crush the meat inside.

3 With your thumbs, press on both sides of the cut, and pull open the shell. Remove the lobster meat in one piece.

2 Remove the meat from the claws, in whole pieces if possible. Discard any membrane attached to the meat.

CHICKEN MISO RAMEN

Quick, easy to make, and beautifully satiating, chicken miso ramen is an everyday type of dish. The fermented, salty miso pairs exceptionally well with a chicken stock base, and the white soy sauce adds a delicate depth to the dish.

Prep time 10 mins **Cook time** 10 mins **Yield** 4 bowls

6 cups **Chicken Stock**

¼ cup white miso paste

1 TB. white soy sauce

2 tsp. sake

1 tsp. sesame oil

½ tsp. granulated sugar

24 oz. (680g) fresh **Ramen Noodles**

4 **Marinated Soft-Boiled Eggs**, sliced in half lengthwise

½ cup scallions, finely chopped

2 bok choy bulbs, sliced in half lengthwise and blanched

1 cup cooked corn kernels

1 In a large pot over medium heat, bring Chicken Stock to a simmer.

2 Add white miso paste, white soy sauce, sake, sesame oil, and sugar. Simmer for 5 minutes.

3 In a large pot of boiling water over high heat, cook Ramen Noodles for 50 seconds, stirring occasionally. Drain, rinse, and divide between 4 deep serving bowls.

4 Fill the bowls with hot broth, just covering noodles.

5 Neatly arrange Marinated Soft-Boiled Eggs, scallions, bok choy, and corn on top of noodles in each bowl.

CHICKEN SHIO RAMEN

The garlic and ginger really come through with this traditional, clear, salt-based broth. All of the toppings are light, delicate in flavor, and work well with the broth.

Prep time 15 mins   **Cook time** 20 mins   **Yield** 4 bowls

6 cups **Chicken Stock**

4 garlic cloves, crushed

1 2-in. (5cm) knob ginger, sliced

1 TB. sake

2 TB. mirin

1½ tsp. kosher salt

24 oz. (680g) fresh **Ramen Noodles**

4 **Marinated Soft-Boiled Eggs**,
   sliced in half lengthwise

½ cup scallions, finely chopped

½ cup **Menma**

1 cup bean sprouts, blanched

1 cup beech mushrooms, trimmed

4 sheets nori

1 In a large pot over medium heat, bring Chicken Stock, garlic, and ginger to a boil. Reduce heat to low, and simmer for 10 minutes.

2 Strain broth, discarding garlic and ginger. Return broth to the pot and add sake, mirin, and kosher salt. Simmer for 5 minutes.

3 In a large pot of boiling water over high heat, cook Ramen Noodles for 50 seconds, stirring occasionally. Drain, rinse, and divide between 4 deep serving bowls.

4 Fill the bowls with hot broth, just covering noodles.

5 Neatly arrange scallions, Menma, bean sprouts, and beech mushrooms on top of noodles in each bowl.

6 Tuck 1 nori sheet into broth on the side of each bowl, leaving a corner sticking up over the top of the bowl.

BUTTER CORN CHiCKEN RAMEN

Rich, hearty, and utterly delicious, this ramen is perfect when the nights begin to get a little chilly. Make this ramen in late summer, when fresh corn is at its sweetest. The contrast of the sweet corn and salty miso is a real winner.

Prep time 15 mins **Cook time** 20 mins **Yield** 4 bowls

6 cups **Chicken Stock**

1 TB. minced garlic

1 TB. minced shallots

¼ cup white miso paste

1½ tsp. granulated sugar

8 slices **Chasu Pork Belly**

1 tsp. kosher salt

24 oz. (680g) fresh **Ramen Noodles**

4 **Marinated Soft-Boiled Eggs**, sliced in half lengthwise

½ cup scallions, finely chopped

2 cups cooked corn kernels

4 small pats butter (about 2 TB.)

¼ cup sesame seeds

1 In a large pot over medium heat, bring Chicken Stock to a simmer.

2 Add garlic, shallots, white miso paste, and sugar. Simmer for 10 minutes.

3 While broth is simmering, heat a large sauté pan over high heat.

4 Sprinkle Chashu Pork Belly with kosher salt, add to sauté pan, and sear on both sides for 2 minutes each.

5 In a large pot of boiling water over high heat, cook Ramen Noodles for 50 seconds, stirring occasionally. Drain, rinse, and divide between 4 deep serving bowls.

6 Fill the bowls with hot broth, just covering noodles.

7 Neatly arrange Marinated Soft-Boiled Eggs, Chashu Pork Belly, scallions, and corn on top of noodles.

8 Place 1 pat butter on each pile of corn. Sprinkle sesame seeds over bowls.

PEANUT CHICKEN SATAY RAMEN

Inspired by chicken satay, this ramen has a rich broth flavored with peanut butter and curry.

Prep time 4.5 hours   **Cook time** 35 mins
Yield 4 bowls

2 medium fresh chicken breasts

¼ cup plus 1½ TB. soy sauce

2 garlic cloves, crushed

1 tsp. grated ginger

1 TB. light brown sugar

2 TB. lime juice

1 tsp. plus 1 TB. curry powder

1 TB. vegetable oil

1 TB. minced garlic

1 TB. minced ginger

1 TB. granulated sugar

6 cups **Chicken Stock**

1 cup crushed tomatoes

¾ cup peanut butter

¾ cup coconut milk

2 tsp. crushed chili flakes

1 tsp. kosher salt

24 oz. (680g) fresh **Ramen Noodles**

4 **Marinated Soft-Boiled Eggs**

½ cup cooked corn

1 red bell pepper, thinly sliced

¼ cup cilantro

4 lime wedges

Special Equipment:

8 bamboo skewers

Grill

1. Pat chicken breasts dry with a paper towel. Cut chicken into strips approximately 3 to 5 inches (7.5 to 12.5 cm) long and 1 inch (2.5cm) wide.

2. Prepare marinade. In a large bowl, mix ¼ cup soy sauce, crushed garlic, grated ginger, light brown sugar, lime juice, and 1 teaspoon curry powder. Place chicken strips in marinade. Refrigerate for 2 to 4 hours.

3. Soak the bamboo skewers in cold water for 20 minutes so they don't burn when on the grill.

4. Take chicken strips out of marinade and divide among the bamboo skewers. Set aside.

5. Prepare broth. In a large pot over medium-high heat, heat vegetable oil. Add minced garlic, minced ginger, sugar, and remaining 1 tablespoon curry powder. Cook for 1 minute, stirring constantly.

6. Add Chicken Stock, crushed tomatoes, peanut butter, remaining 1½ tablespoons soy sauce, coconut milk, crushed chili flakes, and kosher salt, and bring to a boil. Reduce the heat, and simmer for 15 minutes.

7. Grill chicken skewers for approximately 5 minutes on each side, depending on thickness. Set aside.

8. In a large pot of boiling water over high heat, cook Ramen Noodles for 50 seconds, stirring occasionally. Drain, rinse, and divide between 4 deep serving bowls.

9. Fill the bowls with hot broth, just covering noodles.

10. Arrange 2 skewers of chicken in each bowl, as well as Marinated Soft-Boiled Eggs, corn, red bell pepper, and cilantro. Serve with lime wedges.

CHICKEN MARSALA RAMEN

Italian and Japanese cuisines share a similar love of pasta and noodles, so why not marry some of the flavors? Mushrooms and marsala wine complement each other perfectly and give an Italian feel to this ramen dish.

Prep time 15 mins   **Cook time** 35 mins   **Yield** 4 bowls

2 TB. butter

1 cup fresh shiitake mushrooms, sliced

1 cup fresh oyster mushrooms, sliced

1 TB. minced garlic

2 TB. minced shallots

1 TB. fresh thyme, pulled from stem and finely chopped

1 cup dry marsala wine

4 cups **Chicken Stock**

2 cups **Tonkotsu Pork Stock**

2 tsp. kosher salt

¼ cup fresh lemon juice

1 tsp. granulated sugar

24 oz. (680g) fresh **Ramen Noodles**

4 **Soft-Boiled Eggs**, sliced in half lengthwise

1 cup cooked chicken, shredded

2 TB. scallions, finely chopped

1 In a large pot over medium-high heat, melt butter. Add shiitake and oyster mushrooms, and cook for 5 minutes, stirring occasionally.

2 Add garlic, shallots, and thyme. Cook for 3 minutes, stirring constantly, until juices have evaporated.

3 Add dry marsala wine to the pot, and deglaze by scraping up any bits on the bottom. Cook for 5 minutes, or until liquid is reduced by half.

4 Add Chicken Stock and Tonkotsu Pork Stock, and bring to a boil over high heat.

5 Reduce to a simmer over low heat and add kosher salt, lemon juice, and sugar. Simmer for 10 minutes. Taste and adjust seasonings, if necessary.

6 In a large pot of boiling water over high heat, cook Ramen Noodles for 50 seconds, stirring occasionally. Drain, rinse, and divide between 4 deep serving bowls.

7 Fill the bowls with hot broth, just covering noodles. Neatly arrange Soft-Boiled Eggs, chicken, and scallions on top of noodles in each bowl.

RECiPES WiTH PORK STOCK

You'll find you can build hundreds of variations of ramen with rich, creamy tonkotsu pork stock or quick pork stock. From pairing tonkotsu stock with the sea flavors of bonito, to creating a pork red curry ramen, the possibilities are endless!

TONKOTSU PORK STOCK

Making your own pork stock is an incredibly rewarding labor of love. During the cooking process, you'll see the stock go from clear to milky-white, due to the breakdown of collagen in the pork bones being absorbed into the stock. The stock isn't seasoned, which will give you the freedom to season your ramen according to each recipe.

Prep time 45 mins   **Cook time** 12 hours
Yield 2 to 3 quarts (2 to 3l)

Ingredients:

4 pig feet (ask your butcher to cut them in quarters)

2 to 4 smoked hocks (optional)

2 lb. (1kg) pork thigh bones

2 lb. (1kg) chicken bones

1 lb. (450g) pork back fat

2 yellow onions, sliced in half and ends removed

1 3-in. (7.5cm) knob ginger, skin on

4 leeks, roughly chopped and cleaned

2 large carrots, roughly chopped (no need to peel)

1 cup garlic, crushed

3 bunches scallions (about 15 to 20 stems), ends removed

2 Granny Smith apples, quartered

Special Equipment:

Large colander and cheesecloth

Chopstick or knife

Fine-mesh skimmer

1 Place pig feet, smoked hocks (if using), pork thigh bones, chicken bones, and pork back fat in a large stockpot, and cover with water. Let sit for at least 1 hour to help remove blood and impurities.

2 Strain bones into a large colander, and discard water. Place bones back in the pot and add fresh water, just covering bones.

3 Place the pot on the stovetop over high heat. Just before water boils, remove the pot and drain bones in the colander again. Rinse each bone under the faucet, ensuring you remove all of the blood and dark matter. Use a chopstick or knife for this purpose.

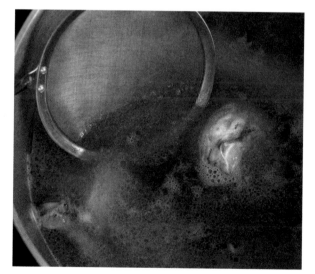

4 Once cleaned, return bones to the pot and add at least 4 quarts (4l) water, ensuring bones are submerged. Bring to a boil over high heat. Skim stock with a skimmer for at least 30 minutes to remove any gray scum. Place a fitted lid on the pot, and boil for 6 hours.

5 In a large pan over high heat, char cut side of yellow onions and ginger until black and fragrant.

Continued ➡

6 Add charred onions and ginger, leeks, carrots, garlic, scallions, and Granny Smith apple quarters to stock. Keep at a low boil for 5 hours. Stir bones every 45 minutes to ensure they don't brown.

7 Strain the stock using a fine-mesh strainer, or a colander with a cheesecloth, and discard solid bits. Stock is now ready to be used immediately.

Storage: Allow stock to cool, and then transfer it to a sealable container. You can store it in the refrigerator for no more than 1 week or in the freezer for up to 6 months.

Pork Stock

QUiCK PORK STOCK

This quick stock is clear and light but will still provide a lovely pork-flavored base for your ramen soups. Like the previous pork stock recipe, the stock isn't seasoned, which will give you the freedom to season your ramen according to each recipe.

Prep time 20 mins **Cook time** 2.5 hours **Yield** 2 to 3 quarts (2 to 3l)

1 Place pork bones in a large stockpot, cover with cold water, and bring to a boil over high heat. Just before water boils, drain bones in a colander, rinse them, and return them to a cleaned pot. Add at least 2 quarts (2l) fresh water.

2 In a dry pan over high heat, char yellow onions and ginger. Add charred onions and ginger, carrots, garlic, scallions, and tart apples to the pot.

3 Place the pot on the stovetop over high heat, and bring to a boil. Reduce heat to a low boil, and cook for 2 hours.

4 Strain stock, and discard solid bits. Stock is now ready to be used immediately.

Storage: Store this stock in the same way as the primary pork stock. if freezing, freeze in individual portions or ice-cube trays for easy use.

Ingredients:

3 lb. (1.5kg) pork bones

2 yellow onions, roughly chopped

1 2-in. (5cm) knob ginger, sliced

2 large carrots, roughly chopped (no need to peel)

½ cup garlic, crushed

1 bunch scallions (5 to 10 stems), roughly chopped

2 tart apples (such as Granny Smith), quartered

Special Equipment:

Large colander

Skimmer

Quick **Pork** Stock

BARBECUE PORK TSUKEMEN

Inspired by traditional American barbecue dishes, this dipping ramen has a smoky barbecue flavor accompanied by two favorite barbecue sides—corn and greens!

Prep time 15 mins **Cook time** 25 mins **Yield** 4 bowls

24 oz. (680g) fresh **Ramen Noodles**

3 cups **Quick Pork Stock**

1½ TB. mirin

3 TB. soy sauce

¼ cup barbecue sauce

1½ tsp. black vinegar

¾ tsp. crushed chili flakes

4 scallions, finely chopped

2 tsp. kosher salt

1 TB. lemon juice

1 bunch (about 5 stems) mustard greens, stemmed and chopped

1 TB. vegetable oil

12 slices **Chashu Pork Belly**

4 **Marinated Soft-Boiled Eggs**, sliced in half lengthwise

1 cup cooked corn kernels

½ cup **Menma**

Special Equipment:

8 serving dishes or bamboo mats

4 deep serving bowls

1 In a large pot of boiling water over high heat, cook Ramen Noodles for 50 seconds, stirring occasionally. Drain, rinse, and divide between 4 serving dishes or bamboo mats.

2 In another large pot over medium heat, heat Quick Pork Stock. Add mirin, soy sauce, barbecue sauce, black vinegar, crushed chili flakes, and scallions. Simmer for 10 minutes.

3 In a medium pot over high heat, boil 5 cups water, 1 teaspoon kosher salt, and lemon juice. Once water is boiling, add mustard greens, and cook for 5 minutes. Drain and set aside.

4 In a large sauté pan over medium-high heat, heat vegetable oil. Sprinkle remaining kosher salt over Chashu Pork Belly. Sear it in the pan on both sides, about 2 minutes on each side. Remove from the pan and set aside.

5 Fill 4 deep serving bowls with broth. Divide Chashu Pork Belly, Marinated Soft-Boiled Eggs, corn, mustard greens, and Menma between 4 serving dishes or bamboo mats.

6 Serve each guest a bowl of broth, a dish of noodles, and a dish of garnishes.

SPICY MISO PORK RAMEN

Packed with umami, this hearty dish offers up a pleasing bowl of ground pork, pungent red miso paste, and fiery chili flakes. Chili black bean paste—a medium-hot mixture of black beans, chili, vinegar, and sesame oil—provides a spicy tang to the dish and complements the pork.

Prep time 15 mins   **Cook time** 25 mins
Yield 4 bowls

6 cups **Quick Pork Stock**

3 TB. chili black bean paste

2 tsp. rice wine vinegar

1 TB. granulated sugar

3 TB. red miso paste

2 TB. vegetable oil

1 TB. minced garlic

8 oz. (225g) ground pork

2 TB. soy sauce

1 tsp. crushed chili flakes

24 oz. (680g) fresh **Ramen Noodles**

4 **Marinated Soft-Boiled Eggs**, sliced
   in half lengthwise

½ cup cooked corn kernels

2 scallions, finely chopped

2 tsp. **Burnt Garlic Oil**

4 sheets nori

1 In a large pot over medium heat, bring Quick Pork Stock to a simmer.

2 Add chili black bean paste, rice wine vinegar, sugar, and red miso paste. Simmer for 10 minutes.

3 While broth is simmering, heat a large sauté pan over medium-high heat, and add vegetable oil.

4 Add garlic and ground pork to the pan, and cook until meat begins to brown, about 3 to 5 minutes.

5 Add soy sauce and crushed chili flakes to ground pork mixture, and cook for 3 minutes until cooked through. Turn off the heat and set aside.

6 In a large pot of boiling water over high heat, cook Ramen Noodles for 50 seconds, stirring occasionally. Drain, rinse, and divide between 4 deep serving bowls.

7 Fill the bowls with hot broth, just covering noodles.

8 Arrange ground pork, Marinated Soft-Boiled Eggs, corn, and scallions on top of noodles in each bowl.

9 Drizzle Burnt Garlic Oil over each bowl. Arrange 1 nori sheet along the side of each bowl, halfway in broth.

BONiTO PORK RAMEN

Bonito flakes, a staple in Japanese cooking, lend a savory, salty flavor to this pork-based ramen. This land-and-sea combination of bonito and pork creates a dish that's simple and delicious.

Prep time 20 mins   **Cook time** 20 mins   **Yield** 4 bowls

6 cups **Tonkotsu Pork Stock**

4 tsp. soy sauce

2 tsp. kosher salt

1 TB. mirin

1 TB. sake

1/3 cup bonito flakes, tightly packed

8 slices **Chashu Pork Belly**

1 TB. vegetable oil

24 oz. (680g) fresh **Ramen Noodles**

1/2 cup fresh radishes, thinly sliced

1/2 cup beech mushrooms, trimmed

1/4 cup scallion greens, thinly sliced

4 sheets nori

1 In a large pot over medium heat, bring Tonkotsu Pork Stock to a simmer.

2 Add soy sauce, 1 teaspoon kosher salt, mirin, sake, and bonito flakes. Simmer for 10 minutes.

3 In the meantime, heat vegetable oil in a large sauté pan over medium-high heat. Sprinkle remaining 1 teaspoon kosher salt over Chashu Pork Belly. Sear in the pan on both sides until golden, about 2 minutes for each side. Remove from the pan and set aside.

4 In a large pot of boiling water over high heat, cook Ramen Noodles for 50 seconds, stirring occasionally. Drain, rinse, and divide between 4 deep serving bowls.

5 Strain broth, discarding bonito flakes. Pour hot broth into each of the serving bowls, just covering noodles.

6 Neatly arrange Chashu Pork Belly, radishes, beech mushrooms, and scallions on top of noodles in each bowl. Arrange 1 nori sheet along the side of each bowl, halfway in broth.

SWEET-AND-SOUR SPiCY PORK RAMEN

Borrowed from the Chinese, this dish has pineapple juice, which gives the broth its sweet-and-sour flavor, as well as fiery chili garlic sauce.

Prep time 15 mins **Cook time** 25 mins **Yield** 4 bowls

6 cups **Quick Pork Stock**

6 TB. red miso paste

1½ tsp. black vinegar

1 TB. chili garlic sauce

1 tsp. granulated sugar

½ cup pineapple juice

1 TB. vegetable oil

8 oz. (225g) ground pork

1 TB. minced garlic

2 TB. soy sauce

1 tsp. crushed chili flakes

24 oz. (680g) fresh **Ramen Noodles**

½ cup **Menma**

4 **Marinated Soft-Boiled Eggs**, sliced in half lengthwise

½ cup scallions, finely chopped

4 sheets nori

1 In a large pot over medium heat, bring Quick Pork Stock to a simmer.

2 Add red miso paste, black vinegar, chili garlic sauce, sugar, and pineapple juice. Simmer for 10 minutes.

3 While broth is simmering, in a large sauté pan over medium-high heat, heat vegetable oil.

4 Add ground pork and garlic to the pan. Cook until meat begins to brown, about 6 to 8 minutes.

5 Add soy sauce and crushed chili flakes, and cook for 3 minutes, until cooked through. Turn off the heat and set aside.

6 In a large pot of boiling water over high heat, cook Ramen Noodles for 50 seconds, stirring occasionally. Drain, rinse, and divide between 4 deep serving bowls.

7 Fill the bowls with hot broth, just covering noodles. Add cooked pork to each bowl.

8 Neatly arrange Menma, Marinated Soft-Boiled Eggs, and scallions on top of noodles in each bowl. Arrange 1 nori sheet along the side of each bowl, halfway in broth.

TONKOTSU RAMEN

One of the most famous and well-loved ramen varieties, tonkotsu is rich, silky, complex, and extremely satisfying.

Prep time 20 mins   **Cook time** 15 mins   **Yield** 4 bowls

6 cups **Tonkotsu Pork Stock**

1 TB. sake

2½ tsp. kosher salt

½ tsp. sriracha

2 tsp. mirin

½ tsp. granulated sugar

1 TB. vegetable oil

8 slices **Chashu Pork Belly**

24 oz. (680g) fresh **Ramen Noodles**

4 **Marinated Soft-Boiled Eggs**, room temperature and sliced in half lengthwise

4 slices narutomaki (fish cake)

¼ cup scallions, finely chopped

4 squares nori

1 In a large pot over medium heat, bring Tonkotsu Pork Stock to a simmer.

2 Add sake, 2 teaspoons kosher salt, sriracha, mirin, and sugar. Simmer for 10 minutes. (Tip: If desired, you may use the braising liquid from Chashu Pork Belly to season this ramen. Add 2 tablespoons at a time until you achieve your desired level of flavor and saltiness.)

3 While broth is simmering, heat a large nonstick pan over medium-high heat. Add vegetable oil.

4 Season slices of Chashu Pork Belly with remaining ½ teaspoon salt, and add to the pan.

5 Sear on both sides until golden brown, about 2 minutes on each side. Set Chashu Pork Belly aside.

6 In a large pot of boiling water over high heat, cook Ramen Noodles for 50 seconds, stirring occasionally. Drain, rinse, and divide between 4 deep serving bowls.

7 Fill the bowls with hot broth, just covering noodles.

8 Neatly arrange Chashu Pork Belly, Marinated Soft-Boiled Eggs, narutomaki, scallions, and nori on top of noodles in each bowl.

PORK SHiO RAMEN

This dish is a lighter version of tonkotsu ramen made with the Quick Pork Stock. As the title implies, this ramen is salt based. The addition of chicken stock gives it an added complexity in the flavor profile.

Prep time 20 mins   **Cook time** 20 mins   **Yield** 4 bowls

4 cups **Quick Pork Stock**

2 cups **Chicken Stock**

3 TB. white soy sauce

1 TB. kosher salt

3 TB. mirin

2 tsp. granulated sugar

1 tsp. rice wine vinegar

1 cup fresh shiitake
  mushrooms, sliced

24 oz. (680g) fresh **Ramen
  Noodles**

½ cup sliced pickled
  radish

8 slices **Chashu Pork Loin**

4 **Marinated Soft-Boiled
  Eggs**, sliced in half
  lengthwise

½ cup scallions, finely
  chopped

4 sheets nori

1 In a large pot over medium heat, bring Quick Pork Stock and Chicken Stock to a simmer.

2 Add white soy sauce, kosher salt, mirin, sugar, rice wine vinegar, and shiitake mushrooms. Simmer for 15 minutes.

3 In a large pot of boiling water over high heat, cook Ramen Noodles for 50 seconds, stirring occasionally. Drain, rinse, and divide between 4 deep serving bowls.

4 Fill the bowls with hot broth, just covering noodles.

5 Neatly arrange pickled radish, Chashu Pork Loin, Marinated Soft-Boiled Eggs, and scallions on top of noodles in each bowl. Arrange 1 nori sheet along the side of each bowl, halfway in broth.

BACON AND PiCKLED APPLE TONKOTSU RAMEN

Pork and apples are a classic flavor combination in the west, with the sweet, tart apples perfectly balancing the fatty, rich tonkotsu broth. The addition of bacon gives the broth an extra-smoky flavor.

Prep time 1 hour   **Cook time** 30 mins
Yield 4 bowls

1 cup water

½ cup rice wine vinegar

¼ cup plus 1 tsp. granulated sugar

¼ cup plus 1 TB. mirin

2½ tsp. kosher salt

1 4-in. (10cm) strip kombu

1 Granny Smith apple, peeled and thinly sliced

6 cups **Tonkotsu Pork Stock**

5 slices thick smoky bacon, roughly chopped

1½ TB. white soy sauce

1 TB. vegetable oil

24 oz. (680g) fresh Ramen Noodles

8 slices **Chashu Pork Loin,** very thinly sliced

4 **Marinated Soft-Boiled Eggs**, sliced in half lengthwise

½ cup scallion greens, finely chopped

4 sheets nori

1 In a small pot, combine water, rice wine vinegar, ¼ cup sugar, ¼ cup mirin, 1 teaspoon kosher salt, and kombu. Bring to a boil over high heat.

2 Once mixture reaches the boiling point, turn off the heat, and add Granny Smith apple slices. Set aside for 30 minutes.

3 In a large pot over medium heat, bring Tonkotsu Pork Stock and bacon to a simmer.

4 Add white soy sauce, remaining 1½ teaspoons kosher salt, remaining 1 tablespoon mirin, and remaining 1 teaspoon sugar to the pot. Simmer for 10 minutes.

5 Strain broth, reserving pieces of bacon. Set aside.

6 Strain Granny Smith apple slices from pickling liquid, and set aside. Discard liquid.

7 Pat bacon dry. In a medium sauté pan over medium-high heat, add vegetable oil. Add bacon pieces, and fry until crispy. Set aside.

8 In a large pot of boiling water over high heat, cook Ramen Noodles for 50 seconds, stirring occasionally. Drain, rinse, and divide between 4 deep serving bowls.

9 Fill the bowls with hot broth, just covering noodles.

10 Neatly arrange Chashu Pork Loin, Granny Smith apple slices, Marinated Soft-Boiled Eggs, scallions, and bacon pieces on top of noodles in each bowl.

11 Arrange 1 nori sheet along the side of each bowl, halfway in broth.

CUBAN PORK RAMEN

This dish borrows the flavor profile of the popular Cuban sandwich, combining pork, Swiss cheese, and pickled vegetables. Adding Dijon mustard to the broth gives it a little kick that works really well with the pork.

Prep time 20 mins   **Cook time** 15 mins   **Yield** 4 bowls

6 cups **Tonkotsu Pork Stock**

2½ TB. Dijon mustard

2½ TB. soy sauce

1½ TB. mirin

24 oz. (680g) fresh **Ramen Noodles**

8 slices **Chashu Pork Loin**, thinly sliced

¾ cup pickled vegetables

¼ cup scallion greens, thinly sliced

½ cup Swiss cheese, shredded

1 In a large pot over medium heat, bring Tonkotsu Pork Stock to a simmer.

2 Add Dijon mustard, soy sauce, and mirin. Simmer for 5 minutes.

3 In a large pot of boiling water over high heat, cook Ramen Noodles for 50 seconds, stirring occasionally. Drain, rinse, and divide between 4 deep serving bowls.

4 Fill the bowls with hot broth, just covering noodles.

5 Neatly arrange Chashu Pork Loin, pickled vegetables, scallions, and Swiss cheese on top of noodles in each bowl.

CHINESE SAUSAGE AND SCALLOP PORK RAMEN

This is a hearty ramen packed with flavor. Chinese sausage has a lovely sweet pork taste that works well with the mild, creamy scallops.

Prep time 20 mins   **Cook time** 20 mins   **Yield** 4 bowls

---

1 TB. vegetable oil

1 TB. minced shallots

2 cups Chinese sausage, sliced ¼ in. (.5cm) thick

1 TB. minced garlic

4 cups **Quick Pork Stock**

2 cups **Chicken Stock**

1½ TB. soy sauce

2 tsp. sake

2 tsp. black vinegar

2 tsp. granulated sugar

1 tsp. kosher salt

1 cup fresh hen-of-the-woods mushrooms, sliced

10 oz. (285g) bay scallops

2 cups fresh spinach

24 oz. (680g) fresh **Ramen Noodles**

½ cup scallions, finely chopped

4 sheets nori

1. In a large pot over medium heat, heat vegetable oil. Add shallots, and cook for 1 minute.

2. Add Chinese sausage, and sauté for 2 minutes. Add garlic, and cook for 1 minute.

3. Add Quick Pork Stock, Chicken Stock, soy sauce, sake, black vinegar, sugar, kosher salt, and hen-of-the-woods mushrooms. Simmer for 10 minutes.

4. Add bay scallops and spinach. Simmer for 2 minutes, or until scallops have cooked through and are firm to the touch.

5. In a large pot of boiling water over high heat, cook Ramen Noodles for 50 seconds, stirring occasionally. Drain, rinse, and divide between 4 deep serving bowls.

6. Fill the bowls with hot broth, just covering noodles.

7. Evenly divide scallops between the bowls. Sprinkle scallions on top of noodles in each bowl. Arrange 1 nori sheet along the side of each bowl, halfway in broth.

GEKIKARA (SPICY) RAMEN

Gekikara is a spicy ramen packed with flavor. The addition of the chili garlic sauce, along with chili flakes, gives the dish a unique kick. The sautéed leeks balance the heat well and provide a good texture contrast.

Prep time 15 mins   **Cook time** 35 mins   **Yield** 4 bowls

2 bunches leeks (about 6)

1 TB. vegetable oil

1 TB. butter

1 tsp. kosher salt

6 cups **Tonkotsu Pork Stock**

1 TB. sake

1 TB. chili garlic sauce

1 tsp. crushed chili flakes

24 oz. (680g) fresh **Ramen Noodles**

4 **Soft-Boiled Eggs**, sliced in half lengthwise

1 cup cooked corn kernels

½ cup scallions, finely chopped

¼ cup toasted sesame seeds

1 Thinly slice leeks into rings, keeping only white and light-colored green parts. Wash thoroughly in a colander. Drain well.

2 In a large pot over medium heat, heat vegetable oil and butter.

3 Add leeks and kosher salt, and sauté for 20 minutes, stirring frequently, until leeks begin to caramelize.

4 Add Tonkotsu Pork Stock, sake, chili garlic sauce, and crushed chili flakes. Simmer for 10 minutes. Taste and adjust seasonings, if necessary.

5 In a large pot of boiling water over high heat, cook Ramen Noodles for 50 seconds, stirring occasionally. Drain, rinse, and divide between 4 deep serving bowls.

6 Fill the bowls with hot broth, just covering noodles.

7 Neatly arrange Soft-Boiled Eggs, corn, and scallions on top of noodles in each bowl. Sprinkle toasted sesame seeds over the bowls.

PORK RED CURRY RAMEN

Fragrant and bold, this curry dish is flavored with Thai red curry paste and Indian curry powder. The lime juice highlights the curry, and the fish sauce gives the dish depth.

Prep time 15 mins   **Cook time** 15 mins
Yield 4 bowls

1 TB. vegetable oil

1 TB. grated ginger

1 TB. grated garlic

3 TB. Thai red curry paste

2 tsp. medium curry powder

6 cups **Quick Pork Stock**

1½ TB. fish sauce

1 13.5-oz. (390ml) can coconut milk

1½ TB. light brown sugar

1½ tsp. kosher salt

2 TB. fresh lime juice

2 cups fresh spinach

24 oz. (680g) fresh **Ramen Noodles**

10 oz. (285g) **Chashu Pork Loin**, thinly sliced

¼ cup scallions

¼ cup fresh cilantro, roughly chopped

4 lime wedges

1 In a large pot over medium heat, heat vegetable oil. Add ginger, garlic, Thai red curry paste, and curry powder. Cook for 1 minute, stirring constantly.

2 Add Quick Pork Stock, and simmer for 5 minutes.

3 Add fish sauce, coconut milk, light brown sugar, kosher salt, and lime juice. Simmer on low heat for 5 minutes. Taste and adjust seasonings, if necessary.

4 Divide spinach between 4 deep serving bowls.

5 In a large pot of boiling water over high heat, cook Ramen Noodles for 50 seconds, stirring occasionally. Drain, rinse, and divide between the bowls.

6 Fill the bowls with hot broth, just covering noodles.

7 Neatly arrange Chashu Pork Loin and scallions on top of noodles in each bowl. Sprinkle cilantro on top, and serve with lime wedges.

RECIPES WITH VEGETARIAN STOCK

Ramen can and should be enjoyed by vegetarians! Light, fresh, and fragrant, vegetarian stock is a great base for many different types of meat-free ramen dishes, such as tomato miso, curried tofu, and corn chowder.

VEGETARIAN STOCK

This vegetarian stock is light and fragrant, and will provide a good alternative to meat-based stock. Vegetarian stock pairs very well with miso, mushrooms, tomatoes, and corn. Charring onion and ginger will increase their flavor profiles! Do it over an open flame or in a dry pan over high heat.

Prep time 15 mins to overnight   **Cook time** 45 mins
Yield 6 to 7 cups (1.4 to 1.7l)

Ingredients:

2 TB. vegetable oil

1 large yellow onion, roughly chopped

2 celery stalks, roughly chopped

1 2-in. (5cm) knob ginger, sliced

2 leeks, sliced and washed

2 large carrots, roughly chopped (no need to peel)

½ cup garlic, crushed

2 qt. (2l) water

1 cup button mushrooms, roughly chopped

1 bunch scallions (6 to 8 stems), roughly chopped

1 In a large pot over medium-high heat, heat vegetable oil. Add yellow onion, celery, ginger, leeks, carrots, and garlic.

2 Stirring constantly, cook for 10 minutes to caramelize vegetables.

3 Add water and bring to a boil over high heat. Add button mushrooms and scallions, lower the heat to a simmer, and cook for 30 minutes.

4 Allow to cool until it's room temperature, or overnight in a refrigerator to allow maximum infused flavor. Strain stock and discard solid bits.

Storage: Allow stock to cool, and then transfer it to a sealable container. You can store it in the refrigerator for no more than 1 week. This stock also freezes well in an ice-cube tray or 1-cup portions for up to 6 months.

Vegetarian Stock

MUSHROOM MISO VEGETARIAN RAMEN

A light, miso-based soup, this ramen will appeal to mushroom lovers, as it contains three different types. The mushrooms bring an earthy flavor to the ramen, which pairs very well with the tofu and miso.

Prep time 10 mins   **Cook time** 30 mins   **Yield** 4 bowls

6 cups **Vegetarian Stock**

½ cup oyster mushrooms, sliced

½ cup shiitake mushrooms

8 scallions, finely chopped (reserve some green for garnish)

4 TB. vegetarian white miso paste

1 cup firm tofu, cubed

1 cup baby spinach

24 oz. (680g) fresh **Ramen Noodles**

1 cup fresh enoki mushrooms, trimmed

4 sheets nori, sliced into strips

1 In a large pot over medium heat, bring Vegetarian Stock to a simmer.

2 Add oyster mushrooms, shiitake mushrooms, and scallions, and simmer for 20 minutes.

3 Add vegetarian white miso paste, firm tofu, and baby spinach. Simmer for 5 minutes.

4 While broth is simmering, in a large pot of boiling water over high heat, cook Ramen Noodles for 50 seconds, stirring occasionally. Drain, rinse, and divide between 4 deep serving bowls.

5 Fill the bowls with hot broth, just covering noodles.

6 Add enoki mushrooms and nori strips to each bowl.

TOM YUM VEGETARIAN RAMEN

Tom Yum hails from Thailand, and is one of my all-time favorite soups. With its light, creamy texture and citrusy flavor, this dish is balanced and refreshing. You can serve this ramen on a hot summer night with a crisp, cool drink.

Prep time 25 mins   **Cook time** 40 mins   **Yield** 4 bowls

6 cups **Vegetarian Stock**

4 cloves garlic, crushed

2-in. (5cm) knob galangal or ginger, sliced

2 whole stalks lemongrass, peeled and chopped in 3-in. (7.5cm) pieces

3 kaffir lime leaves

2 tsp. Thai chili garlic paste

1 tsp. kosher salt

1½ tsp. granulated sugar

2 TB. white soy sauce

Juice of 1 lime

1 cup oyster mushrooms, trimmed

8 cherry tomatoes

1 cup firm tofu, cubed

½ cup coconut milk

24 oz. (680g) fresh **Ramen Noodles**

¼ cup scallions, finely chopped

¼ cup cilantro, roughly chopped

1 lime, cut into 4 wedges

1 In a large pot over medium heat, bring Vegetarian Stock to a simmer.

2 Add garlic, galangal, lemongrass, and kaffir lime leaves. Cover the pot, and simmer for 30 minutes. Strain broth, discarding solids.

3 Bring broth back up to a simmer and add Thai chili garlic paste, kosher salt, sugar, white soy sauce, lime juice (to taste), oyster mushrooms, cherry tomatoes, firm tofu, and coconut milk. Simmer for 5 minutes.

4 While the broth is simmering, in a large pot of boiling water over high heat, cook Ramen Noodles for 50 seconds, stirring occasionally. Drain, rinse, and divide between 4 deep serving bowls.

5 Fill the bowls with hot broth, just covering noodles. Garnish each bowl with scallions and cilantro, and serve with lime wedges.

TOMATO MiSO VEGETARiAN RAMEN

This ramen is as comforting as a bowl of tomato soup, but with the added depth of salty miso and the addition of delicious, chewy noodles.

Prep time 20 mins   **Cook time** 15 mins   **Yield** 4 bowls

6 cups **Vegetarian Stock**

6 fist-size tomatoes, cored and peeled

1 TB. tomato paste

1 TB. granulated sugar

1 TB. white soy sauce

3 TB. vegetarian red miso paste

2 tsp. fermented chili bean paste

24 oz. (680g) fresh **Ramen Noodles**

¼ cup scallions, finely chopped

1 lime, cut into 4 wedges

1 In a large pot over medium heat, bring Vegetarian Stock to a simmer.

2 Chop tomatoes into bite-sized pieces, and add to broth.

3 Add tomato paste, sugar, and white soy sauce. Simmer for 5 minutes.

4 Add vegetarian red miso paste and chili bean paste. Simmer for 5 minutes.

5 While broth is simmering, in a large pot of boiling water over high heat, cook Ramen Noodles for 50 seconds, stirring occasionally. Drain, rinse, and divide between 4 deep serving bowls.

6 Fill the bowls with hot broth, just covering noodles.

7 Garnish each bowl with scallions, and serve with lime wedges.

COCONUT CURRY TOFU VEGETARIAN RAMEN

Coconut milk and curry powder are a wonderful marriage of creamy and sharp flavors. Lime juice is an important addition that highlights and balances the curry. Cilantro finishes this dish with a bold, fresh flavor.

Prep time 20 mins   **Cook time** 15 mins   **Yield** 4 bowls

6 cups **Vegetarian Stock**

½ cup coconut milk

1 tsp. fresh grated ginger

1 tsp. kosher salt

2 tsp. curry powder

8 button mushrooms, thinly sliced

1 tsp. crushed chili flakes

2½ TB. mirin

1 TB. white soy sauce

1 tsp. granulated sugar

1 cup firm tofu, cubed

1 cup baby spinach

1½ TB. fresh lime juice

24 oz. (680g) fresh **Ramen Noodles**

4 **Marinated Soft-Boiled Eggs**, sliced in half lengthwise

¼ cup scallions, finely chopped

¼ cup cilantro, roughly chopped

1 In a large pot over medium heat, bring Vegetarian Stock to a simmer.

2 Add coconut milk, ginger, kosher salt, curry powder, button mushrooms, crushed chili flakes, mirin, white soy sauce, and sugar. Simmer for 5 minutes.

3 Add firm tofu, baby spinach, and lime juice. Simmer for 5 minutes.

4 While broth is simmering, in a large pot of boiling water over high heat, cook Ramen Noodles for 50 seconds, stirring occasionally. Drain, rinse, and divide between 4 deep serving bowls.

5 Fill the serving bowls with hot broth, just covering noodles.

6 Garnish each bowl with Marinated Soft-Boiled Eggs, scallions, and cilantro.

HOW TO MAKE TOFU FROM SCRATCH

While widely considered a health food, tofu is a staple of both vegetarian and Japanese diets. You can find tofu in many different varieties: silken, soft, firm, and extra firm. Tofu is made from mature soybeans that have been dried (known as daizu), as well as nigari, which acts as a coagulant (solidifier). If you'd like fresh firm tofu to add to your Coconut Curry Tofu Vegetarian Ramen, simply follow these steps.

Prep time 13 hours **Cook time** 20 mins
Yield 14 ounces (400g)

7 oz. (200g) dried soybeans
2 tsp. nigari

Special Equipment:
Food processor
Colander
Finely woven cotton cloth
Soup ladle
$1\frac{1}{2}$-lb. (680g) weight, such as a plate
  (to weigh down tofu)

1 In a large bowl filled with 4½ cups water, soak dried soybeans overnight, about 8 to 12 hours.

2 In a food processor, grind soybeans and soaking water for 2 minutes, or until fine.

3 In a large pot over medium heat, bring 5 cups water to a boil. Add ground soybeans and stir continuously with a wooden spatula. Just before mixture comes to a boil, reduce the heat to low and cook, stirring continuously, for 8 minutes.

4 Line a colander with finely woven cotton cloth, and place over a large pot. Strain mixture through the cloth, and discard solids.

5 Cook soy milk strained into the pot over low heat, stirring continuously with the wooden spatula. When the temperature registers between 150°F and 155°F (66°C and 68°C), remove the pot from heat.

6 In a small bowl filled with 6 tablespoons lukewarm water, dissolve nigari.

7 Add half of nigari mixture to soy milk, stirring with the spatula in a whirlpool pattern. While soy milk is swirling, add remaining half of nigari mixture, stirring gently afterward in a figure-eight pattern. You should notice soy milk beginning to coagulate. Cover the pot, and let stand for 15 minutes.

8 Line a colander with a tightly woven cotton cloth (don't reuse the previous), and set over a bowl that can support it. With a soup ladle, gently transfer coagulated soy milk to the cloth-lined colander.

9 Fold the cloth over top of coagulated soy milk, and place a weight on top. Let stand for 15 minutes.

10 Remove the weight, and gently transfer the bowl to a sink filled with cold water to cool. Once chilled, unfold the cloth, and gently lift out finished tofu.

11 Use tofu immediately, or store in an airtight container with fresh, cold water in the refrigerator for up to 1 week.

CORN CHOWDER VEGETARIAN RAMEN

Fresh, sweet corn is the star of this ramen dish. It's enhanced by the salty, complex flavor of the miso. The addition of half-and-half provides a lovely creaminess to the ramen.

Prep time 20 mins   **Cook time** 15 mins   **Yield** 4 bowls

1 TB. vegetable oil

4 cups **Vegetarian Stock**

1 small yellow onion, diced

1 clove garlic, minced

3 cups cooked corn kernels

2 cups half-and-half

2½ TB. vegetarian white miso paste

2 tsp. mirin

1 tsp. kosher salt

24 oz. (680g) fresh **Ramen Noodles**

4 pats butter (about 2 TB.)

¼ cup chives, finely chopped

Special Equipment:
Handheld immersion blender

1 In a large pot over medium heat, heat vegetable oil. Add yellow onion, and sauté until translucent. Add garlic, and sauté for 1 minute, until fragrant.

2 Add Vegetarian Stock, 2 cups corn, half-and-half, vegetarian white miso paste, mirin, and kosher salt. Simmer for 10 minutes.

3 Using a handheld immersion blender, blend broth until much of corn has been incorporated, while still leaving some larger kernel chunks. Add remaining 1 cup corn, and simmer for 5 minutes.

4 While broth is simmering, in a large pot of boiling water over high heat, cook Ramen Noodles for 50 seconds, stirring occasionally. Drain, rinse, and divide between 4 deep serving bowls.

5 Fill the bowls with hot broth, just covering noodles. Place 1 pat butter in the middle of each bowl, and sprinkle with chives.

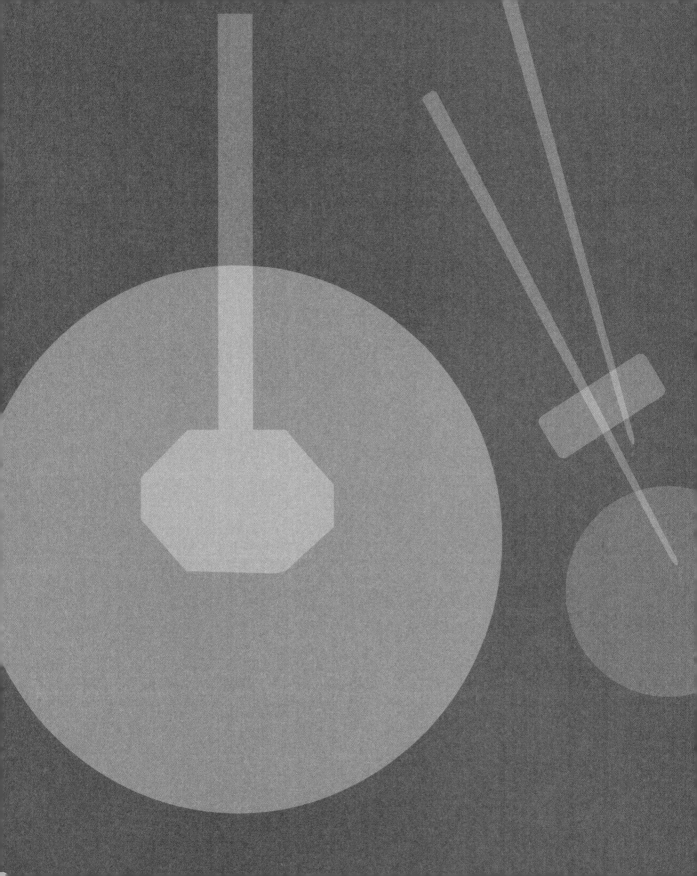

ACCOMPANiMENTS TO RAMEN

While ramen is a dish unto itself, many light, tasty accompaniments can complement a bowl of ramen, such as light salads, edamame, and gyoza.

GYOZA

Gyoza is the Japanese version of Chinese pot stickers. Crisp on the bottom and steamed on top, these delicate yummies will leave you clamoring for more.

Prep time 20 mins   **Cook time** 20 mins
Yield 20 gyoza

4 TB. plus 2 tsp. soy sauce
4 TB. rice wine vinegar
1 garlic clove, minced
1 tsp. grated ginger
3 scallions, green part only, finely chopped
¼ tsp. crushed chili flakes
2 cups green cabbage, finely chopped
½ tsp. kosher salt
5 oz. (140g) ground pork
1 tsp. minced fresh ginger
2 tsp. minced fresh garlic
1½ tsp. red miso paste
1 tsp. sesame oil
1 tsp. mirin
¼ cup cornstarch
20 gyoza skins
½ cup warm water
2 TB. vegetable oil

Special Equipment:

Bamboo steamer
   or double broiler

1 To make dipping sauce, in a small bowl, place 4 tablespoons soy sauce, rice wine vinegar, minced garlic clove, grated ginger, 1 scallion, and crushed chili flakes. Whisk to combine. Set aside.

2 In a large bowl, mix green cabbage and kosher salt. Allow to sit for 15 minutes to draw liquid out. Wrap cabbage in a cheesecloth or thin, clean kitchen towel, and wring it out tightly.

3 Return cabbage to a dry large bowl and add ground pork, minced fresh ginger, minced fresh garlic, remaining 2 scallions, red miso paste, remaining 2 teaspoons soy sauce, sesame oil, and mirin. Mix well with your hands to combine evenly.

4 Lightly dust a baking sheet with cornstarch. Fill a small bowl with warm water. Hold one gyoza skin (flour side facing down) in your palm and pop 1 tablespoon of pork mixture in the center. Dip a finger in warm water, and run it along the outer edge of gyoza skin.

5 Fold over gyoza skin, and pinch it together, making little folds as you go. Make sure to seal it entirely. Place finished gyoza on the floured baking sheet, spacing them out so they're not touching.

6 Spray a bamboo steamer or double boiler with nonstick cooking spray, and then place gyoza on the surface. Steam gyoza over high heat until translucent, about 10 to 12 minutes.

7 Heat a large pan with vegetable oil over medium-high heat. Add steamed gyoza to the hot pan, and brown on both sides, about 2 to 3 minutes per side. Serve with dipping sauce.

EDAMAME

Edamame, otherwise known as soybeans, are widely available frozen in most stores. Lightly boiled and salted, this healthful side dish is a perfect snack or accompaniment to a heavier dish like ramen.

Prep time 5 mins   **Cook time** 5 mins   **Yield** 1 pound (450g) edamame

6 cups water
1 lb. (450g) frozen edamame
½ TB. sea salt

1 In a large pot over high heat, bring water to a boil.

2 Add edamame, and cook for 5 minutes. Drain well.

3 Sprinkle sea salt on edamame, and toss to coat. Serve hot, cold, or at room temperature.

Edamame Serving Tips: You've probably seen edamame as an appetizer at Japanese restaurants. It's great not only as an accompaniment to ramen, but also for adding to ramen and other Japanese dishes in its hulled form.

CUCUMBER-AVOCADO SALAD WITH CARROT-GINGER DRESSING

A perfect summer salad, this dish has a healthful and delicious dressing that is sweet from the carrot and tangy from the ginger. The creamy avocado provides a nice contrast to the crunchy cucumber.

Prep time 5 mins   **Yield** 4 medium salads

2 small carrots, roughly chopped

1 TB. minced shallot

2 tsp. grated ginger

2½ TB. rice wine vinegar

2 TB. vegetable oil

1 tsp. white miso paste (optional)

2 TB. honey

1 TB. water

1 head Bibb lettuce, rinsed

2 ripe avocados, peeled, pitted, and sliced

1 large cucumber, peeled, sliced in half lengthwise, seeded, and sliced

¼ tsp. kosher salt

Special Equipment:

Food processor

1 In the food processor, make dressing by adding carrots, shallot, ginger, rice wine vinegar, vegetable oil, white miso paste (if using), honey, and water. Pulse until well mixed.

2 Arrange Bibb lettuce on 4 plates. Top lettuce with avocados and cucumber.

3 Sprinkle each salad with kosher salt. Drizzle dressing over each salad.

SHISHITO PEPPERS

One out of every 10 shishito peppers is hot (the rest are sweet and flavorful), making eating them a culinary game of roulette! The peppers can be cooked in a variety of ways, including broiled, pan-fried, and grilled.

Prep time 5 mins   **Cook time** 15 mins   **Yield** ½ pound (225g) peppers

1 TB. extra-virgin olive oil
½ lb. (225g) shishito peppers
2 tsp. sea salt
1 TB. fresh lemon juice
1 tsp. shichimi togarashi powder

1 In a large pan over high heat, heat extra-virgin olive oil.

2 Once the pan is very hot but not smoking, turn down to medium heat, and add shishito peppers.

3 Cook peppers for 10 to 12 minutes, tossing them frequently and allowing skins to blister.

4 Once they're done cooking, sprinkle on sea salt, lemon juice, and shichimi togarashi powder. Serve immediately.

Soy-Glazed Shishito Peppers: Mix 2 tablespoons soy sauce, 2 teaspoons honey, 1 tablespoon lemon juice, 1 teaspoon minced ginger, and 1 teaspoon minced garlic. Whisk to combine, and add to peppers after they have been cooking for 5 minutes.

AVOCADO SALAD

Light, fresh, and delicious, this salad is the perfect accompaniment to a hot bowl of ramen. The ginger-vinegar dressing provides a lovely contrast to the creamy avocado.

Prep time 4 mins   **Yield** 4 medium salads

1 TB. vegetable oil

1 tsp. sesame oil

2 TB. rice wine vinegar

2 TB. mirin

1 tsp. grated ginger

1 tsp. granulated sugar

4 to 6 cups mixed greens

2 ripe avocados, peeled, pitted, and sliced in half

2 TB. toasted sesame seeds

1 In a small bowl, place vegetable oil, sesame oil, rice wine vinegar, mirin, ginger, and sugar. Whisk to combine.

2 In a large bowl, toss mixed greens with dressing. Arrange on 4 plates.

3 Neatly fan avocado slices on each salad plate.

4 Sprinkle each salad with toasted sesame seeds.

SPICY BEAN SPROUT SALAD

Simple, crunchy, and spicy, this bean salad has a kick from shichimi togarashi powder, the Japanese seven-spice blend.

Prep time 5 mins   **Cook time** 2 mins
Yield 4 small plates

3 cups bean sprouts

1 TB. sesame oil

1 TB. vegetable oil

2 tsp. soy sauce

1 tsp. shichimi togarashi powder

¼ tsp. kosher salt

¼ cup scallion greens, finely chopped

2 TB. toasted sesame seeds

About Bean Sprouts: Bean sprouts are a common ingredient in Asian cooking. They are often used in stir-fries, in soups, and as a garnish. Plus, sprouted beans require little cooking time.

1 In a large pot over high heat, bring 6 cups water to a boil.

2 Add bean sprouts, and cook for 1 to 2 minutes. Drain in a colander, and rinse with cold water. Set aside.

3 In a medium bowl, combine sesame oil, vegetable oil, soy sauce, shichimi togarashi powder, and kosher salt. Whisk well.

4 Add bean sprouts, and toss to coat evenly. Divide between 4 small salad plates.

5 Garnish with scallion greens and toasted sesame seeds.

RECiPES FOR TRANSFORMiNG iNSTANT RAMEN

If you recall, instant ramen noodles are dried or precooked noodles that are usually eaten after being cooked in boiling water for a few minutes. These noodles are typically sold with a packet of flavoring, such as beef or chicken. While instant ramen has a reputation as cheap fare for college students, these noodles can provide a quick, easy way to put together a meal in no time.

iMPROViNG PACKAGED NOODLES

By simply adding some seasonings and toppings, you can alter the taste of instant noodles to something more flavorful and exotic.

Miso paste, chili garlic sauce, curry powder, vinegar, white pepper, crushed chili flakes, and oils can add some unique flavors to packaged noodles. The ramen can then be topped with quick-cooking vegetables, eggs, or even cured meat (such as bacon or ham) for a full and pleasant taste sensation.

NEW USES FOR NOODLES AND FLAVORiNG

The noodles and flavor packets don't even have to be the base of a recipe. You can also do endlessly interesting things to transform their ingredients into completely different dishes!

For instance, uncooked ramen noodles can be used as a crunchy topping on salads. And recently, intrepid chefs have discarded the noodles and simply used the flavor packet to season their dishes.

From ramen noodle burger buns, to cold salads, to more sophisticated egg dishes, instant ramen is versatile and downright fun to play with.

A NOTE ABOUT THE RECiPES

These recipes use the little bricks of instant noodles with the seasoning packaged in a separate envelope, not the type sold in foam cups. If you're worried about the high sodium that can come from using instant noodles, you can simply discard the flavoring packet.

ASiAN RAMEN NOODLE COLESLAW SALAD

Instant ramen noodles are a great addition to a cold salad. The honey and mango give this salad a touch of sweetness, which is balanced by the tart and sour flavors of the rice wine vinegar and lime juice.

Prep time 20 mins   **Yield** 4 to 5 cups

⅔ cup vegetable oil

1 tsp. sesame oil

¼ cup honey

⅓ cup rice wine vinegar

3 TB. soy sauce

1 tsp. Thai chili garlic sauce

1 TB. lime juice

¾ tsp. kosher salt

¼ tsp. ground black pepper

2 3-oz. (85g) pkg. instant ramen noodles (discard flavor packets)

1½ cups shredded carrots

1½ cups shredded green or red cabbage

1 ripe avocado, peeled, pitted, and diced

1 mango, peeled, pitted, and diced

½ cup roasted cashews

5 scallions, finely chopped

1 In a small bowl, whisk vegetable oil, sesame oil, honey, rice wine vinegar, soy sauce, Thai chili garlic sauce, lime juice, kosher salt, and black pepper.

2 In a large bowl, crumble uncooked instant ramen noodles.

3 Add carrots, green cabbage, avocado, mango, cashews, scallions, and vinaigrette. Toss well to combine.

RAMEN BURGERS

The noodle buns of ramen burgers are crispy on the outside and soft on the inside, and there's a reason they have such a cult following! They're easy to make and utterly delicious, with a spicy ketchup that includes Thai chili garlic sauce.

Prep time 30 mins **Cook time** 15 mins **Yield** 4 burgers

3 3-oz. (85g) pkg. instant ramen noodles (discard flavor packets)

2 eggs

1 tsp. kosher salt

½ tsp. ground black pepper

1 lb. (450g) ground beef

1 TB. soy sauce

1 tsp. sesame oil

1 TB. plus ¼ cup ketchup

4 slices cheddar cheese

2 TB. vegetable oil

1 TB. Thai chili garlic sauce

4 lettuce leaves, any type (optional)

Special Equipment:

8 ramekins (the size you would like your burgers to be)

1 In a large pot over high heat, bring water to a boil. Add instant ramen noodles, and cook until tender, about 3 minutes.

2 Rinse noodles under cold water, drain well, and set aside. Beat eggs in a bowl. Season with kosher salt and black pepper. Add noodles, and stir well to combine.

3 Divide egg mixture between 8 ramekins, squeezing out excess egg, and top each one with plastic wrap, pressing down so the wrap touches noodles. Refrigerate for at least 20 minutes.

4 In a medium bowl, mix ground beef, soy sauce, sesame oil, and 1 tablespoon ketchup. Divide into 4 patties. In a large sauté pan on medium heat, cook patties for 2 to 3 minutes per side, until desired doneness. After flipping burgers to second side, top each with 1 slice cheddar cheese. When cooked, set aside.

5 In the same pan, heat vegetable oil on medium heat. Carefully remove noodles from the ramekins, and fry for 3 minutes on each side, until golden.

6 In a small bowl, mix remaining ¼ cup ketchup and Thai chili garlic sauce.

7 Build your burger! Put 1 ramen bun on each of the 4 plates; top with burger patty, spicy ketchup, and lettuce; and place another ramen bun on top.

RAMEN FRiTTATA

Frittatas are a fantastic breakfast dish and can be made with a variety of your favorite ingredients. The noodles help give the frittata extra structure and a chewy consistency. The flavor packets season the egg mixture, eliminating the need for additional salt and pepper.

Prep time 10 mins   **Cook time** 20 mins   **Yield** 1 large frittata

2 3-oz. (85g) pkg. chicken-flavored instant ramen noodles

8 eggs

1 TB. butter

½ cup button mushrooms, sliced

½ cup chopped ham

¼ cup shredded cheddar cheese

Special Equipment:

Large ovenproof sauté pan

1 Preheat the oven to 375°F (175°C). Boil a pot of water over high heat. Cook instant ramen noodles for 3 minutes, until tender. Strain, rinse under cold water, and drain well.

2 In a medium bowl, whisk eggs and ramen packet flavorings together. Add noodles, and stir to combine.

3 In a large ovenproof sauté pan over medium-high heat, melt butter. Add button mushrooms, and cook for 3 to 4 minutes. Add ham, and stir to heat through, about 1 to 2 minutes.

4 Pour egg-noodle mixture into the pan, and stir with a rubber spatula.

5 Once egg mixture starts to set, sprinkle cheddar cheese on top, and pop in the oven for 6 to 8 minutes, until frittata is puffed and golden. Cut into quarters, and serve immediately.

GLOSSARY

al dente   Italian for "against the teeth"; refers to cooked pasta or rice that's still slightly firm.

all-purpose flour   Flour that contains only the inner part of the wheat grain.

arugula   A spicy-peppery green that has a sharp, distinctive flavor.

assari   A light ramen broth.

bake   To cook in a dry oven.

baking powder   A dry ingredient used to increase volume and lighten or leaven baked goods.

baste   To keep foods moist during cooking by applying a liquid.

beat   To quickly mix substances.

beech mushroom   Named after the trees they grow on, these mushrooms have a bitter taste that can be eliminated with cooking. Once cooked, the mushrooms have a nutty flavor and crunchy texture.

blanch   To place a food in boiling water for about 1 minute or less to partially cook and then douse with cool water to halt the cooking.

black vinegar   An aged vinegar with a rich, woody, fruity flavor.

blend   To completely mix something, usually with a blender or food processor, slower than beating.

boil   To heat a liquid to the point water turns into steam, causing the liquid to bubble. Also, to cook food in boiling water.

bok choy   A member of the cabbage family with thick stems, crisp texture, and fresh flavor.

bonito flakes   Fish flakes used for dashi stock, made from skipjack tuna.

bouillon   Dried essence of stock from chicken, beef, vegetables, or other ingredients. It's popular as a starting ingredient for soups.

braise   To cook with the introduction of a liquid, usually over a period of time.

brine   A highly salted, often seasoned liquid used to flavor and preserve foods. Also, to soak or preserve a food by submerging it in brine.

broil   To cook in a dry oven under the overhead high-heat element.

broth   A stock that has been seasoned and flavored.

brown   To cook in a skillet, turning, until the food's surface is seared and brown in color, to lock in the juices.

caramelize   To cook vegetables or meat in butter or oil over low heat until they soften, sweeten, and develop a caramel color. Also, to cook sugar over low heat until it develops a sweet caramel flavor.

cayenne pepper   A fiery spice made from hot chili peppers, especially the slender, red, very hot cayenne.

chashu   Braised pork loin or pork belly used as a topping for ramen.

chili (or chile)   A term for a number of hot peppers, ranging from the relatively mild ancho to the blisteringly hot habanero.

chili garlic sauce   Also known as sambal, a pungent, spicy condiment widely used in Asia.

chili powder   A warm, rich seasoning blend that includes chili pepper, cumin, garlic, and oregano.

Chinese five-spice powder   A pungent mixture of cinnamon, cloves, fennel seed, anise, and Szechuan peppercorns.

Chinese sausage   A broad term for sausages made in China, the most popular being a thin, sweet, dried sausage.

chive   An herb that grows in bunches of long leaves and offers a light onion flavor.

chop   To cut into pieces, usually qualified such as "coarsely chopped" or with a size measurement such as "chopped into ½-inch (1.25cm) pieces." "Finely chopped" is much closer to minced.

cider vinegar   A vinegar produced from apple cider, popular in North America.

cilantro   A member of the parsley family used in Mexican dishes (especially salsa) and some Asian dishes. The seed of the cilantro plant is the spice coriander.

coconut milk   A nondairy liquid made from grated coconut and water.

coriander   A rich, warm, spicy seed used in all types of recipes.

cornstarch   A thickener made from the refined starch of a corn kernel's endosperm. Before it's added to a recipe, it's often mixed with a liquid to make a paste and to avoid clumps.

cumin   A fiery, smoky-tasting spice most often used ground in Middle Eastern and Indian dishes.

curry   Rich, spicy, Indian-style sauces and the dishes prepared with them. Curry powder is the base seasoning.

curry powder   A blend of rich and flavorful spices such as hot pepper, nutmeg, cumin, cinnamon, pepper, and turmeric.

dash   A few drops, usually of a liquid, released by a quick shake.

dashi   A Japanese stock made from kombu and bonito flakes that's used as a base in many dishes.

deglaze   To scrape up bits of meat and seasonings left in a pan after cooking, usually by adding a liquid such as wine or broth, to create a flavorful stock.

devein To remove the dark vein from the back of a large shrimp with a sharp knife.

dice To cut into small cubes about ¼-inch (.5cm) square.

Dijon mustard A hearty, spicy mustard made in the style of the Dijon region of France.

double boiler A set of two nesting pots that provide consistent, moist heat. The bottom pot holds a shallow amount of water, and the top pot holds the food.

dredge To coat a piece of food on all sides with a dry substance such as flour or cornmeal.

edamame Fresh, plump, green soybeans often served steamed and either shelled or still in the pod.

emulsion A combination of liquid ingredients that don't normally mix well (such as a fat or oil with water) that are beaten together to create a thick liquid. Creating emulsions must be done carefully and rapidly to ensure the particles of one ingredient are suspended in the other.

enoki mushroom Tiny and thin mushrooms, with a small cap. Wild versions can be found in a variety of colors and shapes, while cultivated enoki are bright white and long-stemmed. These mushrooms are mild and sweet in flavor, and rich in antioxidants.

flour Grains ground into a meal. Wheat is the most common flour, but oats, rye, buckwheat, soybeans, chickpeas, and others are also used. *See also* all-purpose flour.

fold To combine a dense and a light mixture with a gentle move from the middle of the bowl outward to preserve the mixture's airy nature.

fry *See* sauté.

galangal A root native to Southeast Asia that's similar in flavor to ginger but more pungent.

garlic A member of the onion family, a pungent and flavorful vegetable used in many savory dishes. A garlic bulb contains multiple cloves; each clove, when chopped, yields about 1 teaspoon garlic.

ginger A flavorful root available fresh or dried and ground that adds a pungent, sweet, and spicy quality to a dish.

gyoza A Japanese dumpling, similar to Chinese dumplings, usually made with pork and cabbage.

hen-of-the-woods A bold-flavored mushroom that resembles the ruffled feathers of a chicken.

hoisin sauce A sweet Asian condiment similar to ketchup made with soybeans, sesame, chili peppers, and sugar.

infusion A liquid in which flavorful ingredients such as herbs have been steeped to extract their flavor into the liquid.

julienne A French word meaning "to slice into very thin pieces."

kansui An alkaline water used to make ramen noodles. Kansui gives the noodles their firm, chewy texture and yellow color.

knead To work dough, often with your hands, to make it pliable so it holds gas bubbles as it bakes.

kombu Edible kelp widely eaten in parts of Asia and used to make dashi stock.

kosher salt A coarse-grained salt made without additives or iodine.

kotteri A rich, thick style of ramen.

marinate To soak a food in a seasoned sauce to impart flavor and make tender, as with meat.

marsala wine An Italian fortified wine, available either dry or sweet.

matsutake A thick and meaty mushroom that can be white or brown. Hard to find and highly prized, matsutakes have a unique, spicy aroma.

menma A Japanese fermented bamboo condiment use to top noodle soups.

mince To cut into very small pieces, smaller than diced, about ⅛ inch (3mm) or smaller.

mirin A rice wine used extensively in Japanese cooking.

mise en place A French term that refers to the preparation of equipment and food before service begins.

miso A flavorful fermented soybean paste, key in many Japanese dishes.

miso ramen A type of ramen made with miso.

narutomaki A Japanese fish cake with a pink spiral in the middle.

nori Edible seaweed.

oyster mushroom With a smooth cap that can grow up to 8 inches (20cm) wide and closely resembles an oyster, this mushroom grows in layers. Subtle in flavor and very versatile, oyster mushrooms tend to soak up the flavor of whatever they are cooked with and have a soft texture.

parsley A fresh-tasting green leafy herb, often used as a garnish.

pinch An unscientific measurement for the amount of an ingredient you can hold between your finger and thumb.

portobello mushroom A large, brown, chewy, flavorful mushroom.

preheat To turn on an oven, broiler, or other cooking appliance early so it will be at the desired temperature when the dish is ready to be cooked.

radish A root crop with a pungent, sweet flavor.

reduce To boil or simmer a broth or sauce to remove some of the water content and yield a more concentrated flavor.

reserve To hold a specified ingredient for use later in a recipe.

rice wine vinegar A mild, sweet vinegar made from rice wine.

roast To cook food uncovered in an oven, usually without additional liquid.

sage   An herb with a slightly musty, fruity, lemon-rind scent and a "sunny" flavor.

sauté   To pan-cook over lower heat than what's used for frying.

scallion   A mild onion with a long green stem, also called green onion and spring onion.

scant   An ingredient measurement directive not to add any extra, perhaps even leaving the measurement a tad short.

sear   To quickly brown the exterior of a food, especially meat, over high heat.

sesame oil   An oil made from pressing sesame seeds. It's tasteless if clear and aromatic and flavorful if brown.

shallot   A member of the onion family that grows in a bulb somewhat like garlic but has a milder onion flavor.

shellfish   A broad range of seafood, including clams, mussels, oysters, crabs, shrimp, and lobster.

shichimi togarashi powder   A Japanese condiment with a variety of spices such as pepper, ginger, seaweed, chili, sesame, and orange peel.

shiitake   A large, dark brown mushroom with a hearty, meaty flavor.

shio ramen   A ramen made with a salt base.

shoyu ramen   A ramen made with a soy sauce base.

simmer   To boil gently so the liquid barely bubbles.

skillet (also frying pan)   A flat-bottomed metal pan with a handle designed to cook food on a stovetop.

skim   To remove fat or other material from the top of a liquid.

soft-boiled egg   A cooked egg with a runny yolk and solid white used to top ramen.

soy milk   Plant milk made with soybeans.

steam   To suspend a food over boiling water and allow the heat of the steam to cook the food.

steep   To let something sit in hot water, as in steeping tea in hot water.

stir-fry   To cook small pieces of food in a wok or skillet over high heat, moving and turning the food quickly to cook all sides.

stock   A flavorful liquid made by cooking meats, fish, and/or vegetables until the liquid absorbs these flavors. The stock is strained, and the solids are discarded. Stock can be eaten alone or used as a base for soups, stews, and so on.

tahini   A paste made from sesame seeds used to flavor many Middle Eastern dishes.

tamarind A sweet, pungent, flavorful fruit used in Indian-style sauces and curries.

tempeh An Indonesian food made by culturing and fermenting soybeans into a cake. It's high in protein and fiber.

teriyaki A Japanese-style sauce made of soy sauce, rice wine, ginger, and sugar.

tofu A cheeselike substance made from soybeans and soy milk.

tonkotsu A thick ramen base made from pork bones that's simmered for a long time.

tsukemen A type of ramen where the broth and noodles are served separately, with the noodles usually at room temperature or cold.

turmic A spicy, pungent yellow root. It's the source of the yellow color in many prepared mustards.

umami The fifth taste after salty, sweet, sour, and bitter. Umami is described as a meaty, rich, and full flavor.

vegetable steamer A perforated insert designed to fit in or on a saucepan to hold food to be steamed above boiling water.

vinegar An acidic liquid often made from fermented grapes, apples, or rice and used as a dressing and seasoning. *See also* black vinegar; cider vinegar; rice wine vinegar; wine vinegar.

wakame Thin seaweed strips used as a ramen topping.

whisk To rapidly mix, introducing air to the mixture.

white soy sauce A thin, clear soy sauce with a delicate flavor. It's produced in a much smaller quantity than dark soy sauce.

wine vinegar Vinegar produced from red or white wine.

wood ear A mushroom that resembles an ear, wrinkled and floppy in appearance. These are typically used because of their crisp texture rather than their taste.

zest Small slivers of peel, usually from citrus fruit such as a lemon, lime, or orange.

iNDEX

ABOUT THE AUTHOR

NELL BENTON owns The National Café, located in the Walker's Point neighborhood in Milwaukee, Wisconsin. The café, which she purchased in 2010, specializes in fresh, locally sourced dishes with an international flair. Born to a British mother and American father, Nell grew up in Los Angeles, California, and Green Bay, Wisconsin, with frequent trips to visit relatives in Devon, England. Her formative years were spent following her mother and grandmother around the garden and kitchen.

After collecting a degree in anthropology/sociology at St. Norbert College in De Pere, Wisconsin, Nell spent almost a decade living and working all over the world, which fueled her passion for international cuisine. After stints in Indonesia, Egypt, and England, Nell obtained a culinary degree from The Art Institute of Fort Lauderdale, Florida. She travels often to Asia to further her knowledge of Asian cuisine.

ACKNOWLEDGMENTS

I can't sufficiently express my deep gratitude to my hardworking, overeducated, kind-hearted café staff for their unwavering support and willingness to take over many of my duties, allowing me to focus on this book: Angela Wierzbinski, my manager; Meg Shecterle, my assistant manager; Arielle Yanasak, my catering manager; Julia Borden, my beverage manager; Victor Hernandez; Mandi Hollis; Dan Bernath; and Ashley Parrill. Thank you for helping me love what I do!

To my friend and chief recipe tester, Chef Thi Cao: thank you for the endless hours in the kitchen helping me test recipes, play with flavors, and roll out noodles. There's no one I love cooking with more.

A huge thank you to Michael and Shelly Diedrick. Without their generosity and kindness, I wouldn't have my café.

A heartfelt thank you to my editor, Nathalie Mornu, for her time, expertise, and patience in going through each page of the book with me.

There are many people who have helped me along my culinary journey and given me a hand in getting my business off the ground. Scott and Marjorie Moon, Clare Norton, Tom Crofts, Nigel LeQuesne, Chef Kevin Guay, Barbara Benton, David Turnpaugh, Andrew Bruce, Sean Henninger, Gary and Denise Wierzbinski, Joe Sutter, Amanda Joy, and Jax: without your support, I would not be where I am today. My heartfelt thanks.

Finally, to my amazing family, thank you for everything. To Mary Maloney, my twin sister and other half, for her steadfast support and encouragement; Robert Maloney, my amazing and inspiring brother; Anna Benton, my older and wiser sister; my nieces, Violet and Helena, for making me laugh and recognize the importance of play; and my parents, Jim and Helen Benton, who have filled my life with their grace, love, encouragement, and support. Thank you!

Alpha Books and DK would like to thank the following people for their hard work and dedication in making this book: Ronnie Andren, photography assistant; Kanisorn Sinprasert and Carolyne Hilario, food styling assistants; Ruthy Kirwan, recipe tester; Dave King, additional photography; and Lucy-Ruth Hathaway, additional food styling.

The publisher would like to thank the following for their kind permission to reproduce their photographs: 22-23 iStockphoto.com: Illustrious (map)

All other images © Dorling Kindersley

For further information see: www.dkimages.com